# How to Get a Grip

## Coping Strategies for Complicated Times

David P Bullis, PhD

BALBOA.PRESS
A DIVISION OF HAY HOUSE

Balboa Press books may be ordered through booksellers or by contacting:

Balboa Press
A Division of Hay House
1663 Liberty Drive
Bloomington, IN 47403
www.balboapress.com
844-682-1282



Print information available on the last page.

ISBN: 978-1-9822-7927-1 (sc)
ISBN: 978-1-9822-7929-5 (hc)
ISBN: 978-1-9822-7928-8 (e)

Library of Congress Control Number: 2022901909

Balboa Press rev. date: 09/20/2022

# CONTENTS

Wrapping Up

# DEDICATION

This book is dedicated to two people. First my paternal grandfather H Edmund Bullis, who led the way by working on issues of Mental Hygiene after he came back from Europe in World War II. He pioneered the idea that mental and emotional wellness are things that can be taught and supported rather than the results of some luck of birth or right of wealth and power. Although we never got the chance to talk about how he saw the world or how our views would have aligned or differed, his example has always stayed with me, and I write this book with fond memories of the time we shared together.

This book is also dedicated to my mother Anne Bullis whose sage words when I was a child helped name this book. My sister and I rarely argued when we were kids but occasionally, we would get on each other's nerves. On one specific occasion we must have gotten on my mother's nerves as well. She raised her voice and told us to stop bickering and "get a grip" on ourselves. My sister and I fell over laughing at the instruction (likely my mother's aim from the start). It was good advice then and I have followed it personally and professionally ever since. When I was thinking about titles for this book, her advice seemed like a good summary of the techniques that will follow. It was certainly a better title than "Stop Bickering!" So, if you've ever felt like life is getting on your nerves, read on and learn how to get a grip!

# PROLOGUE

So, before we get started it would be helpful to get a sense for yourself what the specific areas of stress are in your life. On the next page you can see the Get a Grip Stress Inventory. This is a very general attempt at describing the various areas of stress that impact people's lives. For each category there are some examples of what typically falls within that heading. In the left most column, there is space to write in your specific challenge or concern. This scale is simply to mark the areas that you will be focusing on finding coping tools for. The higher the level of stress the higher the level of need to address it. Multiple areas of minor stress, however, can also be targets for change since it all adds up over time. The items listed are obviously not a comprehensive list of all the things that stress people out, so I added one row at the bottom for you to add in whatever specific challenge you feel gets in your way the most.

# GET A GRIP STRESS INVENTORY

| Sources of Stress (Specific) | Not at all Stressful 1 | Kind of Stressful 2 | Clearly Stressful 3 | Majorly Stressful 4 | Severely Stressful 5 |
|---|---|---|---|---|---|
| Physical health (illness, injury, disease, capacity, endurance, resilience) | | | | | |
| | | | | | |
| Mental Capacity (memory, attention, concentration, thinking, focus) | | | | | |
| | | | | | |
| Emotional Health (worry, sadness, anger, frustration, anxiety, depression) | | | | | |
| | | | | | |
| Spiritual Capacity (faith, spirituality, connection to a higher power) | | | | | |
| | | | | | |
| Partner relationship (spouse, partner, boy/girlfriend, best friend) | | | | | |
| | | | | | |
| Family Relationships (parents, siblings, extended family, in-laws) | | | | | |
| | | | | | |
| Social Relationships (friends, neighbors, colleagues, acquaintances) | | | | | |
| | | | | | |
| Community relations (neighborhood, village, town, city, region) | | | | | |
| | | | | | |
| Environment (pollution, access to nature, urban, suburban, rural) | | | | | |
| | | | | | |
| Work (stability, income, unemployment, obligations, responsibilities) | | | | | |
| | | | | | |
| Financial (monthly bills, medical debts, short-term and long-term savings) | | | | | |
| | | | | | |
| Other (anything else that you can think of that causes you stress) | | | | | |
| | | | | | |

# HOW WE WORK

*Chapter 1*

# INTRODUCTION

*"Reality is the leading cause of stress for those who are in touch with it."* Lily Tomlin.

"You are a real foul weather friend," my friend, Sarah, said one cold and rainy night in our first year of college. She was having boyfriend troubles and I was listening. I may not have been her first choice, but since I was the only psychology major, in a group of engineers, I was the guy most likely to get it. In the end, I didn't have much useful advice to offer, beyond being a good listener, but Sarah seemed much happier when she left. I realized, often just talking about our problems with someone we trust helps us get through rough times. Over the past 25 years as a psychologist, I have found helping others feel understood and normalizing their challenges can go a long way toward reducing stress. We've all had those days, weeks, or months when we've felt stressed out and benefitted from having a shoulder to cry on or someone to vent to.

Unfortunately, the reason we're stressed doesn't just go away after we've blown off steam, by ourselves or with a nearby listener. We can change our attitude about the stress but that doesn't change the source of the stress. While it may be true that our attitudes shape our actions, we still need to take those actions to reduce our stress and that takes something more. I am generally positive about positive affirmations, but I think it is important to put some muscle behind our desire to feel better. We need tools to help us realize that we're not powerless in how we respond to the situations we are in. This book is my attempt to give you those tools.

One of the challenging aspects of giving advice about coping with stress is that there is no single cause of it. Some things are universal, like "illness is stressful" and some are specific to only us, "why is my friend Dan ghosting me?" What is stressful for one person could be invigorating for someone else. One person's hobby is another person's catastrophe. We also have our own ways of dealing with stress. Some people manage stress by actively taking on the source while others hunker down and wait it out. Some techniques encourage others to help us, and many others are unseen, or unrecognized, by those around us. Given that we each have our own version of what stresses us out and our own set of skills for how we deal with it, there can never be a one-size-fits-all strategy for managing stressful events in our lives.

Another challenge with writing a book on stress management is that the sources of stress change over time and are different in cities from what they are in rural areas, as well as for people with more resources as compared to people with fewer resources. Over the years that I have been writing this book, I have been following a stress survey put out by the American Psychological Association. They have done a survey for years that tracked what the top causes of stress are in America. In 2009, the survey (American Psychological Association (2009). *Stress in America: Mind/Body Health: For a Healthy Mind and Body, Talk to a Psychologist,* Stress in America™ Survey™) found the top five stressors to be money (71%), work (69%), the economy (63%), family responsibilities (55%), and relationships (51%). Fast forward 10 years the survey showed the top source of stress were mass shootings (71%), access and cost of health care (71% for people with private insurance and 53% for people with public insurance), acts of terrorism (60%), the natural climate (56%), and the political climate (56%) (American Psychological Association (2019). *Stress in America: Stress and Current Events.* Stress in America™ Survey). Just one year later, the majority of American's reported elevated stress levels (67%) and the focus of our stress was mostly on the coronavirus pandemic (78%) followed by health care (66%), mass shootings (62%), climate change (55%) and rising suicide rates (51%) (American Psychological Association (2020). Stress in America™ 2020: A National Mental Health Crisis).

The surveys show that there is no fixed set of stressors in our lives. The sources are different for different people, and they change over time in keeping with the events surrounding us. It should be noted that those surveys only captured the stress of the people who took the time to respond to the questions. We may never know the true depth and breadth of what causes stress in the lives of all Americans, or other people throughout the world. There will always be hot button issues grabbing the headlines but they will keep changing over time.

How can *Get a Grip* help? The chapters in this book all have concepts aimed to help you deal with stress in a variety of ways. The examples will be related to specific problems, like job changes and health crises, but the techniques could be applied to any stressful challenge. These concepts have arisen out of my experiences working over the years with many different people in many different settings, so my hope is that you will be able to make use of them no matter what your particular struggle point is. But first, some background concepts to keep in mind.

The first thing to remember is that our emotions are normal. They happen for a reason that is usually related to the situation and our mindset at the time. Our emotions are not an illness that needs to be fixed, avoided, or numbed, nor do we need to judge them as weird, wrong, or shameful. All too often our society makes it seem like our emotions are a sign of mental illness or weakness. This tendency is at the root of so many political and advertising campaigns for fad diets and medications and other quick fixes. Our emotional reactions always relate to what we think is going on around us. To be clear, our thoughts about what is going on can be wrong or mistaken, but our emotional reaction is not. This is the basic idea behind why we react so strongly to horror movies even though we know they are not real. Facing our feelings, as a normal part of who we are, will allow us to feel more in control over what is happening, not less.

Second, there are several ways to think about the ideas in this book. You can think about these concepts in terms of scale, ranging from you as an individual to community groups or even organizations. The concepts are all illustrated using individual people's struggles, but larger groupings often face similar issues, albeit with more people or more complex problems. Try to imagine how team leaders might use some of the same concepts to steer their organization in a healthier direction. You can think of the techniques in terms of time, whether you are taking on a task in the present or building toward something bigger in the future. You can pick one technique or idea and try to make the most out of that or use the whole group of ideas like a multi-pronged tool. You can use the ideas in any way that works for you and what you want to achieve. You can work your way through the book in order if that helps you build your coping plan or jump from chapter to chapter to get ideas.

Third, people in the middle of stressful situations always ask when are things going to get back to normal? The answer is Yes, you will get to a normal state again, but it will be a new normal, that may or may not look like the old normal you are used to. That new normal will not come just with the passage of time ("next year things will be normal again") nor is it a place on a map you can go to ("if i can just find the right place than things will get back to normal"). The new normal is more of a way of thinking and seeing the world, and your challenges, in a new way. The contents of the following chapters hopefully will give you the tools you need to see your situation in that new way, hopefully healthier, more balanced, and sustainable over time.

Fourth, to illustrate the ideas I'm describing and how the concepts would work in real life, I use case histories that are composites of actual clients I have worked with over the years. You will meet Brad, Darlene, Eliot, Alex, Samantha, and Clara. These "characters" are diverse in age, gender, education, income levels, and problem type. Although they are not actual individuals, the problems, and solutions, they illustrate are real. I've given each of them names and a brief back story, but any similarity between them and people you may know is purely accidental. I hope you can find aspects of each of the characters to be relatable and think about how their coping strategies could be applied in your life. I tried to strike a balance between giving too many intense details while still giving enough to make their stories relatable. If you feel like the story is pulling up too many strong emotions for you, skip the story part and focus more on the solutions. By the time you're done reading I hope you will feel like you have new tools to help you cope with the stressful situations in your life. A coping plan takes time and the more tools you have the more solid the plan is likely to be.

Lastly, about that Stress Inventory. The items on that checklist represent the common areas of stress my clients have focused on over the years. As you begin this journey of healing, just take note of where you are starting from, don't worry about what the "score" is. Look at the areas that you carry the most stress in because those are going to be the targets of your eventual coping plan. As we saw with the Stress in America surveys, those areas of stress may well change, but after you have gone through the book and mastered the coping skills that follow, (oh yeah!) you will be able to make a coping plan that is custom fit for you. I have put another Stress Inventory at the end of the book so you will have an opportunity to go over the same items in the follow-up and show yourself just how much more skilled you are then.

So, the book is organized in a way to help you develop a coping plan customized to you. The first section lays out a foundation for how we think, that we will build upon. The second section is focused on the specific ideas and techniques that make up the coping model. The third section is devoted to the importance of balance in our lives and a few different ways of thinking about it. The fourth section is the wrap-up where we focus on how to put all the ideas together into a coping plan that will work for you. I threw a few extra ideas into the Appendix, that are not unique to the coping model, but make a good addition to any plan for overall wellness. At the end of each chapter is a "Now You Try It" section with a templated form you can use to practice how that chapter's concept works on your particular problem. By the end of the book you will have a collection of tools that you will be able to apply to your specific stressor. Those tools will be what you use to make the coping plan that is customized to your needs. No one's plan is likely to look like anyone else's, even yours might well change over time, but each one will fit the needs for the person who designed it. This is exactly how it should be.

Let's get started.

*Chapter 2*

# A SELF IN FOUR PARTS

We're all unique and complicated people. We have different aspects of ourselves, and those parts can be thought of in several different ways. Understanding how these parts can add up to be more than the whole can be useful in helping us cope with life's challenges. In this chapter we are going to think of our core characteristics as being organized in four distinct layers, much like you might picture in a column on an ancient Greek temple or on the front of a bank or library. The bottom layer is the physical, followed by the mental (thinking) layer, then the emotional, and finally the spiritual.

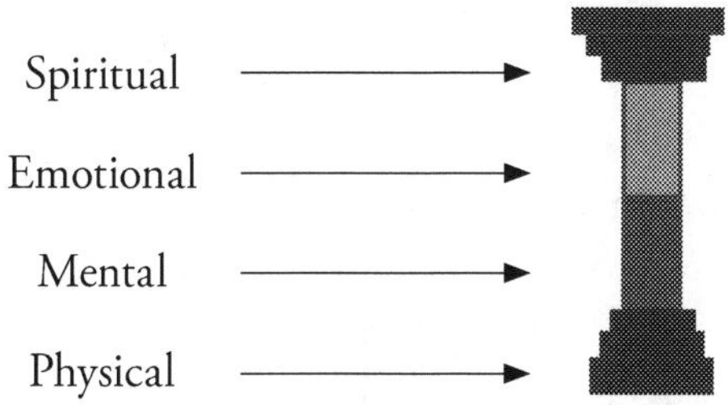


Each layer is distinct, yet interrelated, and the pillar's full height is reached through the contribution of each layer, much in the same way, our full sense of self is a combination of all four layers. We have strengths and weaknesses at each layer and learning what they are, and how to make use of them, can be a huge benefit to our coping skills and health. But first, to give the coping conversation some real life context I would like you to meet Brad.

Brad and his wife Sarah married after they graduated from high school. He worked free-lance in construction, going from job to job, to support the family and Sarah worked part-time at the school where their two children went. The building jobs started to dry up as the economy shifted after the nearby factories closed. The financial strain put a lot of stress on their marriage, and they separated for a bit. Frustrated with his situation, Brad, 35 years old at the time, joined the Army Reserves to make some extra money so he could support his wife and 3 and 11-year-old children. Despite not having extensive military training he was sent to Iraq to work on re-building programs, and he was glad to be using his skills for a good cause. One day, while driving to a job site with his crew, his unarmored truck ran over an old unexploded bomb left over from the war. Brad survived but suffered multiple physical, mental, and emotional injuries. He was honorably discharged and sent home to heal and get on with his life, such as it was. He had to learn how to live his life with disabilities and he had a lot of decisions to make about how to adjust and what to do next.

### The Physical Level

The bottom layer, the physical, is the most basic because none of the other layers could exist without it. Literally, if our physical body stops working, we would not survive. It doesn't matter how smart, emotionally sensitive, or spiritually in touch we are, the physical body is the vehicle that carries us wherever we go. But even short of the extreme, a structurally weak or unstable base layer jeopardizes the integrity of the whole column. We know this because when we don't feel well physically, it is harder to think straight, we may be more emotional, and we don't have the energy to reflect on our larger spiritual path. This base layer includes all the obvious aspects of our health, including our strength, endurance, capacity, and pain level. It also involves how well our vital organs, like our bowels, bladder, brain, heart, and lungs, are functioning. When we have stress, we often notice it first in the muscle tension in our shoulders or back, or a headache or upset stomach. Not to sound too much like "a psychologist" but our bodies are "wise" and register stress even before we are aware of it consciously. Our brains come pre-wired for expressing and processing emotion from birth. Newborn babies get their needs met purely through the emotional expressions of crying and cooing, long before they know how to say what they want, and our brains keep that capacity throughout our lives.

Brad's story is a good example of how important the base physical layer can be. When he first woke up in the hospital after the explosion, his brain and body were beaten up and not working normally at all. Initially, he didn't recall anything about the explosion or even what he had been doing the week before. He was in a complete daze and could not recall thinking or feeling anything during that time. The medical staff were a bit surprised, at first, to see that he didn't have much of an emotional reaction to what had happened. He responded to questions about it all as if the whole thing was boring him. He had been brought up with a strong spiritual faith and was actively involved in his church back home, but he seemed disconnected from his spirituality as well, being equally unmoved when the pastor came to visit and prayed for his recovery.

The reason for Brad's reactions (or lack of reactions) was that, in addition to the obvious physical injuries to his legs, his brain had sustained significant damage as well. Also, after several surgeries on his legs, he was on a lot of medication for his pain and blood pressure problems, so the healing process was interfering with his ability to think or feel normally. Most of his treatment and healing in those first several weeks was focused on his physical recovery. It didn't seem to matter to him that he had an effective treatment plan or that he was surrounded by attentive staff. Until his brain and body started to heal, he was unable to appreciate any of those higher-level aspects of his life. Brad's injuries are a dramatic example of how our physical health affects all the other levels of our being since the brain is the seat of all awareness and reactivity, but the pain and the blood pressure were central in determining how he felt day to day.

Every coping plan needs to start with this understanding of the importance of our bodies' functioning. Our physical functioning often underlies why we're feeling like we do and starting at that level can also give us some options for how to feel better. For example, early on in Brad's recovery, there were times when he looked like he was resisting treatment because he got upset about being restricted to the unit and not being able to walk on his own due to his instability. His brain was not able to calmly process what his own capacity was, at first, nor what his pain-relief needs were. Once he got on a regular medication routine and rest periods were interwoven into his schedule, he was able to cope better. These interventions were based on his physical needs primarily since his mental capacity and emotional and spiritual aspects of his life were not fully accessible to him yet.

Even if we don't have a specific disease or injury, our physical realm still is the most basic. If we've been so singularly focused on work that we've stopped eating healthfully, or aren't getting enough sleep or daily exercise, our bodies can get worn down and we will be too tired to work to our full capacities. The early symptoms of stress are often felt in our stomachs, chest, or back and shoulder muscles. Our bodies are the vehicles that carry us through life, so a primary coping strategy is paying attention to, and responding to, any physical signs or indicators of stress, to make sure that vehicle is in top condition. If our physical health is as strong as possible, we'll have more success managing the other levels of self since we'll have that base of support to rely on.

**The Mental Level**

The second level is the mental level. It represents all aspects of our thinking: how we think, what we think about, what we understand about our situation, how we plan, our memories and our expectations. Our thoughts can easily get overloaded when we are confronted by new situations, good or bad--when we first learn about a new diagnosis, hear that we're pregnant for the first time, get fired, or get a big promotion. The shock of hearing the initial information often interferes with our ability to pay attention or think much about what follows. This normal self-protection trick kicks in when we have too much to absorb because our brains can only process a certain amount at any one time, much like a cup that can only hold so much water. This is most obvious with big issues like these health and finance examples, but it also happens in less dramatic ways. Think about people talking on their cell phone while driving or texting while walking in the middle of a busy shopping area. When we divide our attention, we give only partial thought to each activity and the more activities going on at the same time the less energy and focus we can devote to any one of them. The CDC, for example, reported in 2018, that 2,841 people died in motor vehicle crashes involving a distracted driver, so this is not a trivial matter. (www.cdc.gov/motorvehiclesafety/distracted driving/index.html)

Much of our time and energy is spent focusing on this thinking level and it is not bound to a certain time frame like our physical level is. While we feel our physical sensations right now (pain, temperature, strength, and weakness) our thoughts can also wander to the past or the future. We review how the sales meeting went last week or focus on planning what customers we need to see today, thinking about where to go to dinner tonight or what our kids are going to do next summer. We have no limits on what topics or time frames we can think about.

In addition to our own daily mental tasks, we now also have the 24-hour news cycle with information coming at us from all angles. We're often mentally absorbing stuff from the radio, television, streaming services, social media, and list serves, all on easily accessible devices. Some of this may be necessary for work or for maintaining our social networks, but it can also be a way to escape and avoid reality. Some of us have a bigger appetite for information than others, so there is no "one size fits all" diet of information.

When we get unwelcome news in our lives, most of us go online and search for information about what do about it. Unfortunately, the internet holds both the best and the worst information and it can be very difficult to tell the difference in times of stress. When people first learn they have cancer, for example, they often go online to research their disease and find out what others are saying about it. They may come away thinking they're going to die at any second or that they should start drinking orange juice out of a left-handed cup every other Wednesday because someone in a chat room claimed it cured them. Neither outlook is true or helpful. There are many reputable sites out there with very useful information but mostly to prompt questions for the professionals rather than provide any definitive answers. At our clinic we make a point of telling patients right up front that we don't recommend doing online research, but we still give them the reputable sites with the right information. We understand everyone needs information (and having a sense of control) but we want them to get the helpful, rather than potentially harmful information.

So, since our mental level can be both a source of strength and weakness, what are the coping tools to help prevent us getting overloaded? One technique is to make a set of "rules" that we follow whenever we start to get overwhelmed. Folks in the military would call these "rules of engagement." Thinking out ahead about how to respond when we're getting upset makes responding easier. One of the oldest methods in the book is to "count to 10" whenever we feel our emotions rising. This works because it gives us time to get over our initial emotional reaction and come up with a more well-thought-out response. In real life, simply counting to 10 is not usually going to be enough time, but certainly having a rule like, "I don't respond to any intense email within 5 minutes of getting it," would go a long way toward reducing the number of "flaming emails" we're sending out because we're stressed.

One of the central tenets of the type of therapy I use the most (cognitive behavioral therapy) operates at this level of self. The central premise of CBT is that feelings affect our thoughts and behaviors and changing how we think will give us more control over those feelings and behaviors. A core CBT technique is to notice and then take a step back from our automatic emotional thoughts and reactions. Taking a "reality check" allows us to see if what we're thinking is based on what is really happening in that moment or if we're reacting based on some flawed perception of what is happening. Once we're aware of the actual situation, we're in a much better position to act appropriately.

These were tools Brad used a great deal as he was healing. He learned that when he had too many things going on in one day, his body would be tighter and he would feel less flexible, both mentally and emotionally. His "rules of engagement" related to who he listened to and how he organized his time. He learned to shut off his electronic devices for parts of the day so he wouldn't feel flooded with too much information. He relied on a few "trusted advisors," namely his doctor, a trusted physical therapist, and his closest family members, to sort out the few information outlets that he should be paying attention to. Together they all helped Brad learn what websites and support groups would give him the best information. He tried to ignore the random suggestions from friends and disgruntled people he met at the hospital or in some of the online chatrooms he was familiar with. He noticed that it helped to be selective about his inputs, but it took a lot of practice because he heard unsolicited opinions all the time.

This strategy can be very helpful, but one potential risk is that we can start listening only to outlets we agree with, leading us down blind alleys at times. We can see this in our politics at times when people only listen to one news outlet and don't get to hear a variety of opinions. We also see it in health care when people only will listen to experts in Western versus Eastern medicine, when both have valuable information to add to the discussion. The best way to avoid getting stuck in an "echo chamber," only hearing what we want to hear, is to be open to other viewpoints and have more than one "trusted advisor." We also need to be clear about what information we take in and what information we choose to leave out, so we can make informed choices and feel in better control. Brad also learned to pace himself by only taking in new information in small chunks. He listened to outside advice on a schedule, reading chat room exchanges a couple of times a day, (like after meals), so the rest of the time he could focus on things he had more control over. He also worked at putting information into notebooks to help keep it organized and get it off his mind, which helped him feel less overwhelmed and better able to focus on other things.

**The Emotional Level.**

Emotions are not just a state of mind that must be suffered through, but rather a way our brains alert us to the events going on around us. Sometimes those events are internal, relating to our physical and/or mental levels of functioning as noted above. Sometimes the emotions are related to challenges that come at us from the outside, such as what is happening in our family, neighborhood, town, city, country, or the world. In fact, it's difficult to describe an emotional experience just in terms of itself. We don't say "I'm afraid because I am feeling fear." We usually reference something that sets off that feeling, like a physical sensation: "I'm really worried about this lump I feel" or a thought: "if my boss hates my presentation, as much as she did last time, she might fire me!" External events can range from the most local--"Why can't my son just pick up his room?!" -- to the most global, "I feel so weighed down by all the hardship I see on the nightly TV news."

Positive emotions have physical and mental aspects as well: "I'm so excited about this promotion I feel like my heart's going to jump out of my chest!!" "I had to sit down when they told me I was cancer free because my legs went numb." We don't tend to think too much or worry about the positive reactions, but they underscore the connections among the body, mind, and emotions just as well as the negative ones do. These connections have been hardwired into the human body from the beginning of humanity, and it's a two-way street. Our anxiety causes our blood vessels to tighten up, our breathing to get more rapid, and our heart to pump harder. Likewise, if we have breathing problems, or are out of shape, we might feel anxious after climbing the stairs because we got out of breath and our heart is pounding. Anyone who has suffered from a broken heart knows the feeling. Even the way we talk about worry shows the relationship between thoughts and worries; we might use such phrases as "racing thoughts" or "having too much on my mind."

Brad wrestled with the interwoven aspects of his physical, mental, and emotional reactions when he returned home to recover. The pain from the physical wounds continued to serve as a reminder of the event long after it was over and, at times, became a mental and emotional barrier in his recovery. Later, when he was back in the relative peace of his hometown, if he heard a truck backfire, his thoughts and body would immediately react like they were back in the war zone. His heart would race, and his muscles would tense up, as if he needed to be ready for action. He immediately started thinking about strategy and counter strike opportunities, as he had been trained to do. This all felt very real to him even though, intellectually, he knew he was sitting in his truck in the grocery store parking lot waiting for his sister to get the groceries. He was suffering from PTSD (post-traumatic stress syndrome), which is a perfect example of how physical, mental, and emotional experiences can all work at the same time. The bulk of our therapeutic work together was focused on helping Brad use those inter-connections to re-wire his brain. He had to learn the signs of physical tension, so he could be better prepared for when he was "ramping up" mentally and emotionally. He learned to "check" his thoughts to make sure he was "in touch with reality" to assure he was reacting appropriately. We came up with a plan to help him stay in control of his reactions, that he followed, and he practiced his calming techniques, which helped him react in healthier ways.

**The Spiritual Level**

Resting at the top of the column is our spiritual self. In a sense, this is the culmination of all the other levels. It's dependent on our physical self to exist and is a hybrid of our mental and emotional selves. How we think of this spiritual level often depends on our cultural traditions. In some cultures, spiritual practices have evolved to focus on rules of conduct, while in others the spiritual practices are more focused on making sense of one's place in the world and managing hardships. Most religions include aspects of both, and each person has his or her own personal take on the balance between the mental and emotional aspects of their faith. In many cases, this includes a belief in God or a higher power, but even if you're not religious, this top level can serve as a way to connect to something bigger than yourself. That could be with the natural world outside, a professional group related to your career, or even a shared life experience, like being a cancer survivor. One can have more than one "spiritual home," and how we define our spiritual place can be as unique as we are as people. One of my spiritual homes is being by the ocean, so I try to be there as often as I can.

The spiritual level may not arise out of an experience that we initially embrace but it can come to serve our needs. As Brad found when he first struggled with the label of "disabled vet" he didn't know where he fit in the world he used to know. He had never had to navigate the world with such a clear label on himself. At first, he relied on his family since they were his first spiritual home, but they didn't fully understand what he was going through at each level of his recovery. He later joined a veteran's support group and did some events that raised awareness for wounded warriors, which helped him feel less alone. Over time, he realized that his place in the world had only deepened as he found a cause bigger than himself to give his time and energy to.

**Putting it all together**

Taken in total then, the picture of the self as four levels illustrates how and why we act, think, and feel the way we do. In addition to helping us better understand our physical, mental, and emotional reactions, it can also lead to ways of coping with those reactions. Since each of the levels both affects, and is affected by the others we have a variety of ways of tackling challenging reactions. Starting at the bottom of the column, as noted at the beginning of this chapter, one of the first signs we are overloaded is how we feel in our bodies. Those initial sensations may be physical, but we use our mental awareness to notice them. We tend to focus on the physical sensations first because they grab the most attention and, only later, do we take the time to think through what the implications of those sensations are. It's like when a severe storm fills the first floor of your house with five feet of water; you don't tend to think about the specifics of your home insurance policy or what color you want to paint the walls when you rebuild, you are just focused on survival.

Once that physical level has gotten our attention then we become more attuned to our thoughts. That is when we start to ruminate on whatever is annoying us. Brad noticed that he would often wake up with his head in an endless loop, thinking about the day of the explosion and all the sights, smells, and sounds that seemed etched into his memories. These worrisome thoughts would often keep him up at night, only adding to his list of worries, since he needed a good night's sleep to get through the rehabilitation therapies. As he worked on his recovery, at every level, he came to see how the fear and anxiety, related to the initial loss of control from the blast, was driving the thoughts and magnifying the physical issues. It was through all this work of healing that he found the company of other veterans, who had been through what he had, so important to putting himself "back together." That additional spiritual home was key to his eventual full recovery.

When we are using the pillar to understand how we think and feel it is important to look at both the positive and negative sides of each level because each level has assets and liabilities. At first, Brad focused mostly on the negative side of the column. He thought about the daunting nature of the physical recovery because the damage was obvious, by the looks of what he had lost, and permanent in the sense that his legs would never be the same. He could see how much he had to learn (mental) about regaining his strength and capacity, new ways of dressing and getting around. He was overwhelmed almost daily with the emotional challenges that were just as daunting as the physical, learning to process and talk about his grief and anger in the therapy. His spiritual home prior to his deployment had been with his church community but in the beginning, he struggled with understanding how the God he had prayed to could let this happen to him. Before he was deployed, he felt, in some ways, like he had a deal with God: if he did the right thing, he would be protected. That was a lot to unpack as he entered the healing phase of his life.

It was on the other side of the pillar that he found what he needed. Once he got started, his physical and occupational therapists worked with his baseline physical strengths, (upper body and cardio) as well as his mental strengths (persistence and singular focus) to push him through the process. He learned to think of his "flashbacks" as a reaction to a non-threatening current event that was based on a prior traumatic event. He then used his physical coping strategies--like burning off his emotional energy with weightlifting--to help him manage the event without spiraling into crisis. He also was more open to getting emotional support from his support group at the Veteran's Administration (VA) Hospital, because they understood where he was coming from. His "support brothers" became a new "spiritual" home and helped him realize that he was not alone with his struggles. Brad maintained his connection to his religious community as well, even though it didn't offer the shared experiences that his support group did, because his faith gave him a deeper connection to his place in the world, which was not something he got from the VA. His loving and supportive family and his sense of humor (emotional strengths) were also crucial to his healing along the way.

Being aware of where and how we feel our stress first can give us a kind of early warning system for when stress is building in our lives and allows us to develop a plan for responding. Our coping strategies are best deployed when we use all four levels described above. Also since each layer of the Pillar of Self has strengths and weaknesses it is easier to see that we don't have to be perfect. This can also be a model for thinking creatively, by using strengths from any one of the layers to overcome weaknesses, or sources of stress, in any of the other layers. The more we can learn to be aware of our stress signals, and not get down on ourselves for feeling that way, the easier it will be to find the strengths we need to overcome the stress, whether it comes from inside us or those around us.

**Now You Try It!** To start off, try paying attention to your body for the next week and see if there is a preferred "signal" sensation that comes with your distress. Does your stress hit you in your gut, does your chest get tight, do you notice the racing thoughts or feelings first? Next, use the Pillar of Self graphic to write out what you think your internal strengths and weaknesses are at each level. Be honest with yourself since these are known only to you. Once you are done, think about ways you might try overcoming a limitation in one area by using strengths in other areas. Also know that the balance of strengths and weaknesses at each level can change over time. You can think about areas you want to make stronger. It can also help to revisit this exercise any time you feel stuck in a stressful situation.

**The Pillar of Self**

Strengths | Weaknesses

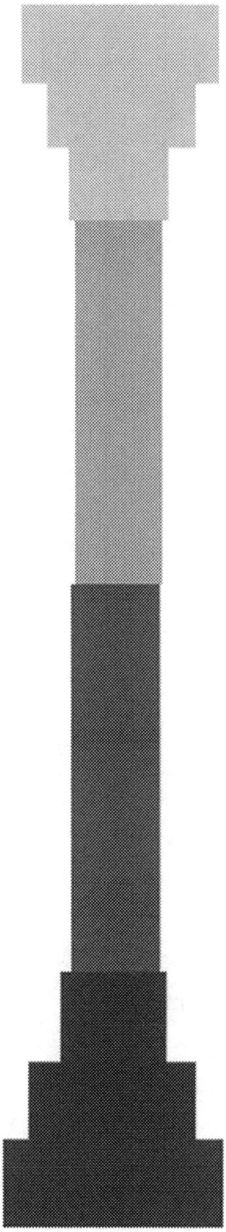

**Spiritual**

**Emotional**

**Mental**

**Physical**

*Chapter 3*

# THE DIAMOND OF SELF

Diamonds come out of the earth like raw stones, rough to the touch. Over time they are processed and cut to have many different sides, or facets. When we rotate a diamond, we only see the light reflecting off one facet at a time, as each side faces a slightly different direction and appears unique. While each facet is distinct unto itself, a diamond is a solid object and not just a "mere collection" of separate parts. We, like diamonds, also have many distinct aspects that are all part of a larger whole. Each facet of us is "cut" over the course of our lives and represents some aspect of ourselves, but no one facet describes all that we are or what we believe. During times of stress, it is not uncommon to get stuck operating out of a limited number of facets, using old habits or behaviors, just doing what we can to get through the day. We sometimes revert to using short-term fixes, like substances or avoidance, to manage an acute phase of stress. These overused routines, that we have done in the past, usually work, but only for a limited time. Unfortunately, we end up holding ourselves back by taking that path of least resistance. Although we may be aware of positives aspects of ourselves, under prolonged stress we can begin to feel fragmented.

Brad felt this way at every level. His body was fragmented by the bomb blast, and he was easily distracted by whatever was happening on the television or out on the street that caught his attention. When he was at the rehabilitation hospital, all he could think about was working through his pain to regain his physical independence. When he got home, his focus shifted to managing life without the structure and routine of the hospital. He found it hard to relate to other people because they had not gone through what he had. His friends and family reminded him that he was still the same strong man he had always been, with "a lot going for him," but he couldn't see that. He didn't feel like the person they remembered. He couldn't get over the idea that he was "damaged goods." Brad felt especially fragmented when he focused on the different facets of himself as if they stood alone, disconnected from his core sense of himself. His rehabilitation was so focused on rebuilding his deficits that he lost track of what his strengths used to be. He struggled to make sense of how his feelings could range so widely, from weakness and anger to happiness and hope, a variability he had never experienced before.

In a sense, we all start out life as undefined and unrefined as a raw diamond. Over time, our life experiences chip away the rough exterior, leaving us with the more defined aspects of who we are. These can be positive, neutral, or negative, but they are all equally real. As Brad began thinking of himself like a diamond, he started to see himself in more realistic terms. He saw all the aspects of himself, both helpful and unhelpful, as representing different facets of who he was, each chiseled out by his journey in life. His facets were unique to him and didn't need to be like anyone else's. At first, he tried to focus only on the healthy parts of his personality, like his work ethic and love of his family, but inevitably he got disappointed when the unhealthy parts, like frustration and irritability due to pain, cropped up. The diamond metaphor allowed him to change his perspective on those shifts. He came to see them less a setback and more as a shifting of focus between equally valid aspects of himself. He started to work on accepting all his facets (even those he didn't want) because he could now see them as just another part of who he was. Knowing that all his facets were chiseled from that same stable core sense of self helped him feel less "damaged."

The diamond analogy also helped give Brad a model for how to respond to present day events. He liked to visualize the diamond as sitting loosely in its setting so it could spin to suit the needs of the moment. He started to make more conscious decisions about which facet he wanted to show the world at any given time. Many people, both friends and professionals, told him that he needed to get over his anger, accept his fate, and move on with his life. Some even told him to focus on being grateful for what he had and stop complaining! Objectively, it's good advice not to be angry all the time but there are times when anger can be useful. When he was in a wheelchair, people would often talk down to him as if he was stupid or simple minded just because he was lower in height than they were. He turned some of the anger energy he felt at those moments into being clear and assertive, speaking up for himself, making people take him more seriously. When he was tired after a day of rehabilitation therapies, he used that same anger energy to push himself to do extra repetitions in the weight room, helping build back the muscle strength that he had lost.

At other times, it was useful to show other facets of himself, like being funny and charming. He got in the habit, when traveling, to prepare the TSA folks by telling them that he was a humanoid robot to explain why he set off all the alarms in the metal detector. It also gave him a chance to show off his robot dance moves. He also felt better about himself as a husband and partner when he could be playful and seductive with his wife as they worked on making their marriage work again. Matching the facet of himself that worked best for the given circumstance allowed Brad to have more success in his interactions. Imagine if Brad had used the same facets in the opposite circumstance, like using his anger energy while trying to get through the airport security or trying to be seductive with his rehabilitation therapists. The facets, in and of themselves, were not bad or wrong but if they didn't match up to the circumstances that he found himself in, things would not have ended well.

When Brad first got home from the service, he experienced a lot of the same problem's other veterans returning from war zones do. He felt he didn't have enough time to decompress or adjust to civilian life. The skills and habits that were essential and potentially lifesaving in a war zone didn't translate well to civilian life. He tried several pre-deployment coping facets first (ignoring it all, drinking a lot of beer, distracting himself) but those were not helping him adjust. He also tried some techniques he learned in the service (getting up a 4 am to work out, issuing orders to those around him, "marching" through his day) but those didn't go over so well with the people closest to him. Brad came to therapy knowing he needed more and different coping skills to better manage his life as a civilian. The sessions helped him see that he had a variety of facets that he could bring to bear on his challenges. He learned to stop judging his facets as bad or good, but rather how some were unhealthy and unhelpful and others much more effective. He learned that when one of the unhelpful facets was in play, he could be more flexible, and switch to a skill that better matched his current circumstances and goals. He used his work ethic, for example, to drive his effort in the rehabilitation therapies and then switched to his "rest and relaxation" mentality when it was time to be calm and read books with his kids. He worked to translate the positive aspects of his service life, like team-work and good communication, into repairing his relationships with his family and friends.

Even if we've never been in a war zone, some of the facets we develop over our lives do not serve us well. Like avoiding difficult situations and hard choices by numbing ourselves with alcohol, tobacco, pain pills, or video games. The challenge is that techniques like having a beer or glass of wine after a stressful day at work or taking ibuprofen for a strained back actually can help over the short run. Over time, however, numbing and avoidance lead to more problems, not less, as we may need more and more to get the same effect. Focusing on quick fixes also doesn't give us an opportunity to practice our healthy skills so they become stronger over time. Knowing that we can switch to a different facet, much like Brad did, also helps us feel more in control. Learning how and when to switch facets is what we do when we practice thinking of ourselves as a diamond. Much like diamonds are one of earth's strongest minerals, our core values are one of the strongest parts of ourselves. The world will probably never stop being stressful but focusing on the many facets that surround our core value allows us the flexibility to respond to whatever life throws at us.

**Now You Try It!** Now make a list of all your different "facets" that you show to the world around you. These may be the same as what you noted in the Pillar of Self worksheet in the prior chapter or they may be very different. When you compare the two worksheets, do they look the same or different. It can be interesting to think about the differences between the version of ourselves that only we see and the version we show everyone else.

| Positive Facets | Diamond of Self | Negative Facets |
| --- | --- | --- |
| | Spiritual | |
| | Emotional | |
| | Mental | |
| | Physical | |

*Chapter 4*

# FOUR THINGS ABOUT EMOTIONS

To illustrate our next concept, I would like you to meet Darlene. Darlene was a 60-year-old divorced woman living in San Francisco, California. Her only child, a 23-year-old daughter, was attending college in Austin, Texas. Darlene had worked hard and risen to become vice president of marketing for a regional retail chain. One day she was told her company had been bought out by a national chain and corporate headquarters was being consolidated in Memphis, Tennessee. She was offered a promotion to a national level job if she moved but her current job was being phased out. She was faced with a lot of choices; she could leave her home and move to Memphis to start an exciting new chapter in her life, or she could leave the company and try to start her career over, which would be difficult at her age. All her friends and supports were in San Francisco, but she would be closer to her daughter if she lived in Memphis. She knew she had to do something because she was too young and vital to retire, and she still had college tuition to pay. Darlene felt a "crazy mix" of emotions and was not sure how to manage them, all while trying to make responsible decisions for herself and her daughter.

Darlene was in a pickle. There were no right answers to her dilemma, and she had multiple priorities to think about. In general, having more choices in life should be a good thing, but as this case shows, it can make life seem difficult as well. At first, she felt like her emotions were all over the map and she did not know what the "right" way to feel was. At times, she felt happy and excited to have a job promotion opportunity and at other times she felt overwhelmed and anxious about all the logistics that went with each choice. What helped Darlene figure her way through this challenging set of decisions was the fact that there are four things we can know about our emotional experience.

**1) Emotions are Normal!** The first step in coping with complicated emotions is to understand that they are a normal reaction to the events that happen to us in life. Emotions, as noted in the Introduction, are not an illness or a problem that needs to be fixed or avoided. Everyone knows the experience of fear, happiness, anger, or joy. How we express those emotions can vary widely between cultures, or even between people in the same family, but everyone expresses their feelings somehow. Because emotions can be uncomfortable, people often try to find ways not to feel them. In some cultures or groups emotions are seen as a sign of weakness, mostly because they remind us of what we don't have control over. People also tend to think about emotional states as being all encompassing, like being in a fog bank, feeling it all around you with no beginning or end in sight. A new way to think about emotions is more like a kind of signal to alert us to events going on around us. Back in ancient times when our ancestors lived with wild beasts out in the woods, emotions helped keep them safe. The people who saw glowing eyes in the tall grass, got scared, and ran away: survived. Their genes were passed down to us. The people that did not pay attention to their emotions and went to see what those glowing eyes were all about ended up as Saber-tooth Tiger Chow: their genes did not get passed down. Most of us do not live amongst the tigers anymore so the stressors may not be as life threatening, but they are no less real. That emotional awareness remains hard wired into our brains. We can see it expressed in pre-verbal babies, as I noted in the introduction, as well as across all cultures and languages.

Darlene struggled with the idea that she was "getting too emotional about all this." She knew she needed to be logical and make the "right" decision for herself and her daughter. She didn't want to allow the emotions to get in the way, but worrying about that only added stress to the very decision she was trying to make. She would wake up in the middle of the night worrying that the anxiety was going to get in the way of her making a good decision, which was a recipe for a terrible night's sleep. Darlene's emotions usually ballooned when she was focusing either on the past or the future. The past typically brought up memories of regrets, missed opportunities, or good times she couldn't re-live. Thinking about the future tended to focus on all the uncertainty of what lay ahead. The past and the future had one thing in common: she had no control over either one. In our work together, we talked about how those feelings (sadness about the past or worry about the future) were not so much "right" or "wrong" as they were a signal that her thoughts had floated to times when she had no control. Once she learned to recognize those signals she could chose to refocus on some aspect of her life where she wasn't so helpless. This allowed her to feel less overwhelmed and better able to think about what to do next.

**2) Energy is a part of every emotion!** Everything we do takes energy. It is like we have one central energy "bank account" to draw from to meet all of our physical, mental, emotional, and spritual needs. Over the course of the day we make many little "withdrawals" to meet our various needs. We replenish that account by getting a good night's sleep, eating well, spending time with people we love, and doing things we find valuable. When our lives are generally stable, we should have a "cushion" of energy left over at the end of the day, or we at least break even, replenishing what we spend each day. Under stressful times, as Darlene noticed, we may spend more energy than we have so even trivial things, like what to eat for dinner, can feel overwhelming. She got embarrassed if she had a mini meltdown at work over stupid things like no paper in the copier. Logically, she knew it did not make any sense, but that only made her frustration worse. It didn't matter whether the exertion was for positive reasons or not. Some days she would be tired physically after a long enjoyable hike. Other days it was because she spent too much mental energy at work trying to figure out her next move. Still other days she was emotionally exhausted after trying to help her daughter manage her own college-related stress in long and intense phone calls. It did not matter if she exerted herself physically, mentally, or emotionally, at the end of the day she felt spent. Once that energy was gone, moreover, she did not have it for anything else.

**3) Emotional energy comes in varying flavors and intensities.** Emotional energy is kind of like barbeque sauce. Every sauce contains some similar elements like oil, vinegar, brown sugar, hot peppers, various seasonings. The assorted flavors and intensities of the sauces are determined by the types and amounts of the ingredients, each to the taste of the chef. Some sauces are mild and may be used in many different dishes by lots of people. Other sauces are intense and only experienced by a few hardy souls. The energy behind our emotions is similar in that every emotion has some but the intensity of the energy and the "flavor" (positive or negative) can be very different. The mild emotions are like when the ketchup takes a long time to come out of the bottle or we hear a song that we like on the radio. We probably would notice the feeling at the time, because it was annoying or pleasant, but it doesn't tend to disrupt our day. We all experience these types and levels of emotions frequently (traffic, weather, the toilet paper running out), but we don't tend to get too upset about them individually. They each take energy to cope with, however, so they can still add up. If you start your day with no milk for your coffee and then get stuck in traffic, and then can't find a parking spot close to the building, while a light spitting rain starts, your energy is getting spent. Later, when your colleague eats the last strudel in the break room you may get more irritated than expected.

When it comes to stronger emotional flavors (think about our feelings about sports teams, musical tastes, food styles, fashion choices) we spend more time and energy on them. We are not focused on these types of feelings all the time, but when we do we are very aware of it. Finally, there are the areas of our lives that we feel very strongly about, and these are what we spend a lot of our energy on. These tend to be our closest relationships, our jobs, hobbies; the things we devote most of our time to. These are the "hottest" feelings and tend to be things we feel we can't live without.

Across the specturm of positive and negative emotions there is this range of intensity. As Darlene noticed, there is rarely a day that goes in only one direction or the other. Even when the day was filled with "little hurdles," both good and not so good things, she could feel exhausted because she had been spending energy in all directions. She could understand how people got burned out because the day to day strain ended up wearing her energy down until she felt like she had nothing left to give. Much like eating 5 alarm chili every day would burn out our stomachs, 5 alarm stress can wear us out as well.

**4) We can control how we spend our energy.** Even on days when everything seems to go sideways, we can use our emotional energy as a source of power that we can channel in healthy ways. If we don't use that energy appropriately, by trying to bottle it up or deny it, it can corrode us from the inside, much like too much hot sauce. We have control over how we spend it as well as how we restore it. To "budget" our energy well, we need to make sure we replenish our energy each day so we will have it to spend when we need it. Much like with our money, we do not necessarily have any control over how much energy we start out with in life or what events will happen to us that will be "costly." All we have control over is how we manage the energy we have and what we "spend" it on. Darlene noticed that when she was well rested and had good energy, she felt able to handle any number of stressful events through the day. When she didn't, then even the mundane things seemed like too much. She recognized the need to get her rest, do some rejuvenating things, and pace herself throughout the day so she was not getting exhausted. At first, she tried staying up late to look up Memphis real estate information online but found she was too tired to work on her big presentations the next day. She found that going to the gym after work burned off some of the emotional stress energy, which allowed her to be less restless at night and get a better night's sleep. She planned her days better knowing which tasks or days were going to take more energy than others. She made different decisions about what she invested her energy in and what she did not. She decided to go to Memphis to check it out because that gave her a better sense of the city then just looking on-line did. She decided not to get involved in any work dramas that came about due to the corporate shake up because they only drained her more.

Some tasks require more energy than others, just like some expenses are bigger than others. Different people may also make different decisions about when and where to invest their emotional energy. Some investments have a direct benefit, like flying to a new city to see if you want to move there and others have an indirect benefit, like listening to your daughter's school life drama's because that helps keep that relationship strong even if the details are not affecting your life directly. Much like our bank accounts, we get to decide how we replenish our emotional resources as well as what we spend that emotional energy on. We are in control over how we use that resource. The uniqueness of people's emotional "spending habits" can explain why some people are bothered by a certain event and others do not seem to be so bothered. Much like our bank accounts, we all start out with different amounts and we have different abilities or opportunities to increase our holdings. Some of us have more expenses that others do and we all make different choices about how we spend whatever is left over after we pay the mandatory bills. The good news about emotional energy, however, unlike actual financial resources, is that we all have the power to improve our emotional resources and find new ways to replenish ourselves and make different choices about the people, places, and things that we are spending our energy on.

**Now You Try It!** As an exercise, try making out an emotional "budget." Use the Energy Budget form on the next page to list the activities or people or things that cost energy for you. In the other column write out the sources of emotional "income" or resources that restore you. As you look at this budget, just like the one you have for your home or work finances, you want there to be more income than outflow. If there isn't, there's a couple of things you can do. One, look for ways to cut back on how much energy you are spending on those people, places, or things that are taking too much from you. Alternatively, try to spend more time with the people, places, and things that restore your emotional energy. More on this later!

| Emotional Energy Budget | |
|---|---|
| Energy Sucks | Energy Boosts |
| | |
| | |
| | |
| | |
| | |

*Chapter 5*

# THE STRING OF LIGHTS

When we're in the middle of a stressful situation we can lose our sense of time. Being overwhelmed now can cause us to remember other times we've felt the same way. If that cycle continues, after a while, we can connect the dots and feel like our lives are one long series of struggles. This happens because memories aren't stored in our brains, as we might assume, in the order events happened. You might expect our early childhood memories to be grouped together, next to our adolescent memories (yikes!), followed by our young adult and then middle-aged memories, and so on. If that were the case though, we would remember those phases of our lives as a mix of the good, the neutral, and the bad. A more helpful model is to think of memories as being organized more around emotional themes then chronological order. If you are in a good mood, you will be more likely to remember positive experiences in the past. If you are in a bad mood, you will be more likely to remember negative experiences in the past. Both would be accurate, but neither would tell the whole story. Emotional memory functions more like a string of holiday lights. Every event that causes a strong emotional reaction gets added to the "string," alongside the other events that share that same emotional flavor. The more often we have a specific emotional experience, the more lights that string would have, and the brighter it would shine. Current events can sometimes trigger memories from far in the past, much like the bulbs at the far end of the string shine as brightly as the ones near the plug. The power for the emotional reaction comes from the present but it lights up our recall of the past. People who have lived through many losses may have more intense feelings of sadness, for example, when the next loss happens. A car backfiring might trigger memories of past explosions to come flooding back, even if we're not currently in a war zone. So, if our brains were like our basements, the boxes of memories lining the back wall would have labels like "sadness", "joy", or "anger" rather than "1975", "2010" or "the high school years."

To illustrate this concept, please meet Alex. Alex was a 25 year-old man who, after graduating from college, started working in his first job as a computer programmer in a local start up. He shared an apartment with friends, who seemed to be enjoying "the good life" working hard and playing hard, but he had trouble joining in. Although he'd always been a worrier, he found the stress of his work and social obligations to be too much. The pressure of meeting deadlines was different than it had been in college because now co-workers and clients were depending on him and there was money on the line. At the same time, his friends were dating and "hooking up" and he wanted to do the same, but it felt forced and out of his comfort zone. He worried about the possibility of getting sick on the way to work or during the workday, sometimes to the point that it was too difficult for him to leave his apartment. His worries interfered with his physical functioning, his thinking abilities, and overwhelmed his emotional capacity. He didn't want to talk about it with any of his friends or his family, so it took months to notice that the worries were taking over his life.

Alex had strong emotional reactions to the social miscues and awkwardness that happend whenever he tried to befriend someone and got rejected. Those present-day negative reactions sent his thoughts reeling back to all the other times he had felt the same way. He had that experience of "connecting the dots." He came to believe that his life was just a series of mistakes and miscues that had led to him being stuck in his current rut. He found that story so convincing that the idea of getting psychological help seemed pointless since his life had always been miserable, was miserable at that moment, and probably always would be miserable. This mindset was hard to argue with since he was remembering actual events in his life, not made up "woe-is-me"- like fantasies. The flaw in his reasoning was that it was not the only story.

Since each emotion has a string of memories attached to it, it's important to notice when we plug and unplug those strings. For example, Alex was so convinced of his negative social skills that he would "plug in" those emotions before he even went out to a bar. He went out expecting things to go badly, which led him to feel awkward, which led him to act awkward, which usually led to the awkward exchange, reinforcing the story all over again. There were other situations when things did not go so poorly but he had so little practice with positive social reactions that he never expected to plug that string in. Part of healthy coping comes from the idea that we can become more aware of which strings we are plugging and unplugging.

First, we need to recognize which emotional string we have plugged in. This may not be as easy as it sounds since, in the heat of the moment, most of us do not think about how we are feeling. Luckily, our bodies send us signals when we're feeling emotional. We can learn what physical sensations come when we are angry, sad, worried, or overwhelmed. Alex's therapy work focused on recognizing when he was holding onto all that tension. He learned his physical discomfort happened every time he plugged in a negative emotional string, reminding him that every trip down "memory lane" was actually a "dead end street." He learned that the pit in his stomach, the tightness in his chest, and the muscle aches in his shoulders started before he went out and got worse as the socializing went along. This awareness was the first step in regaining control over how he responded to the stress, as it was happening, rather than letting it build up and causing him problems later.

That awareness also leads to the second step, which is swapping out the negative string with a different one that changes our experience in the present. The positive and negative emotional strings are all made of equally valid memories, so the choice is more about helpful or unhelpful outcomes, rather than right or wrong. Alex practiced "plugging in" different stories, focusing on past successes when he overcame one obstacle or another. He developed a routine before social events to think out both the helpful and unhelpful strings, like "I will talk to people, and I may even like some of them" and "I will probably be anxious when I talk to them, and they may see that." This side-by-side comparison allowed him to make more conscious decisions to focus on the helpful mind-sets, like "I will talk to the people who make me feel the least anxious and forget about the rest!" Each time he exerted that control he strengthened the helpful "string" by having more examples of when things went well, which in turn made it more likely the next time he faced a social situation.

This string of emotional lights idea is based on how our brains are wired, so don't be surprised if you find yourself thinking about other challenges in the middle of a current one. The current event doesn't need to be the same as the original one for the emotional signals (loss of control, anxiety, anger, regret, etc.) to be triggered. Much of Alex's anxiety related to his own social life but sometimes he felt that way if a group project at work did not go well or he saw co-workers in a meeting that he was not invited to. Even if those work-related events weren't related to him specifically they could still "plug in" the same string of anxiety that his social attempts did. One of the benefits of the String of Lights idea is how it connects our past with our present. Obviously we can't change what has happened in our past but the emotional reactions caused by those events are the same ones "lighting up" now due to the current situation. Understanding how those strings developed helps us shift our thinking from good or bad emotions to helpful or unhelpful ones and allows us to step away from self-judgment. Using our bodily sensations as a signal helps us learn what to plug in or unplug. Pro tip: there can only be one string plugged in at a time. So if you have an unhelpful emotional string active you will not be taking in the more helpful ideas. The reverse is true as well. If we can unplug the sense of anger and powerlessness that will give us an opportunity to plug in the resilience, faith, or perseverence and hope that will get us closer to our goals.

**Now you try it!** Think about the emotional strings you have developed about yourself over the years and then work to develop a list of other strings as well. Try making a few lists that have the heading: "Times when I felt ___________" where you try to remember times when you have been anxious, happy, angry, at peace, etc. Each one will represent an emotional string that later you can plug in, or unplug, depending on the situation. See what you can come up with for a variety of your emotional experiences. Once you have the set you want, think about how you can "plug in" the positive strings more often.

**String of Lights Coping Cards (Sample emotions)**

| Times when I have Felt: <u>Happy</u> |
| --- |
| |
| |
| |
| |

| Times when I have Felt: <u>Sad</u> |
| --- |
| |
| |
| |
| |

| Times when I have Felt: <u>Worried</u> |
| --- |
| |
| |
| |
| |

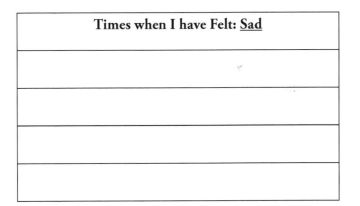

# TECHNIQUES THAT WORK

*Chapter 6*

# CONTROL IS KEY

The importance of being in control is not just an issue for people who worry, like Alex did, it is true for all of us. We can even look at many of the difficulties in society today through the lens of control. Whether we use personal, social, or political actions to regain control or try to escape the pain from a loss of control through substances or other distractions, the effects of our diminished sense of control are a central feature in our society today. Clearly, none of us has absolute power over what happens in our lives, and we all have some level of stress, no matter how successful we are. Though it is true that some people seem to have easier problems, or more resources, that is not the same as coping well. The main difference between coping well, versus not so well, is the degree to which we focus on what we have control over.

Alex's story illustrates some core concepts related to stress. When his life had been more structured and routinized--like it was in college--he had been more emotionally calm and mentally able to focus. Once that sense of order started to slip away, like it did after graduation, he felt his sense of control slipping away as well. The facts of his life had not really changed all that much after he started work. He had the same physical and mental capacities as he had before. What changed were the expectations he felt at his job and the social scene he was a part of.

In Alex's case, he felt the most control when he was at work programming computers, which he was good at. Objectively, knowing the precise language needed to make a computer, or some other machine, do something can be quite complicated. For example, it takes between 500,000 and 600,000 lines of code to run Google Chrome[1]. For Alex, however, coding was easy because he knew the company's computer language and it followed clear rules. He felt the least amount of control when he was trying to manage the unstructured time at work. His co-workers coped with it by playing foosball and scrolling social media during the day and then pulling all nighters to push out the latest software update just before the deadline. It was difficult for Alex to work efficiently when there was no even pacing to the work. The unstructured daily routines, organized only by high stakes deadlines, felt like something he could never get on top of. He saw other people thriving in that start-up culture and felt he must be doing something wrong to be so stressed out all the time. He was quick to point out to me in our sessions, that his colleagues all seemed to cope by an almost equally intense drinking culture, which was also not something he was up for. He didn't tolerate alcohol very well and being drunk made him feel even less in control. Alex felt like he was not able to keep up with either side of the "work hard – party hard" lifestyle.

As that cycle continued, he looked for other areas of his life where he could get some control. He looked to his physical environment and became very controlling over how clean and orderly his apartment looked. He liked his roommates and close friends, all of whom he had known in college, but this inevitably led to some conflicts. Living in a small space with pizza boxes and beer cans regularly thrown around the living room, made it hard to feel like his apartment was a safe place. As his anxiety climbed, he

---

1 https://informationisbeautiful.net/visualizations/million-lines-of-code/

tried to find more ways to manage the home environment by making sure there was no clutter in the living spaces or dishes in the sink because those messes stirred up the "messy" feelings he had inside himself. He kept his own room spotless and almost dustless because he needed at least one space in his life where everything was in its place. His attempt to manage his stress only made matters worse by magnifying the social anxiety, a cycle that continuously fed on itself.

Socially, Alex wanted very much to fit in and be like everyone else was. Like at work, however, he had trouble figuring out how to deal with the unstructured time. In theory, talking to people his age should have been simple. He knew a lot of the people who hung out in the same places he and his friends went and he didn't have any trouble talking to people in non-social settings, like the grocery store. He knew he was capable, but he felt pressured to be funny or clever like his roommates were. Alex also felt awkward talking to people in bars and navigating the dating scene, especially since he was attracted to both men and women but did not feel accepted by either group. It only took a few missed cues and rejections for his old anxiety to rear its ugly head. He could further compound his stress by thinking about all the things he didn't have control over, which led him to feel even more helpless, angry, and frustrated. Because the social scene caused the most anxiety, he stayed in a lot, which was part of why he wanted the apartment to be a calm refuge from the world.

Prior to being in therapy, most of Alex's attempts at finding more control, through working harder or forcing himself to be social, or ignoring it by drinking more or isolating himself, only led him to feeling progressively more out of control. He was following a maddening pattern where searching from more control only led to more stress as each attempt inevitably failed because he was trying to control the wrong things. When Alex and I talked about coping with anxiety we focused on how he felt less stressed out when he was in control of a situation, like computer coding, despite how objectively hard that situation might be and he felt the most amount of stress when he felt the least amount of control, even with "simple" things like talking to people socially.

As you know from the introduction, Alex's anxiety was a normal reaction to thinking he was out of control. Once he stopped thinking he was "less than" when his anxiety came up, Alex learned what to do to help himself cope better. He worked hard to find ways to feel more in control of his situation. So, he wouldn't be distracted by sounds in the break room, he chose music he liked to listen to on his noise cancelling ear pods when he was at work. He set goals for his work routines every day, so he was not up against deadlines at the last minute. He started an exercise regimen every day to help him burn off some of that anxious energy. He chose to go to game nights at a local coffee house rather than the chaotic bar scene, so he was able to socialize in smaller groups, in quieter settings, with more social rules to follow. He even got his roommates to accept a house cleaning rotation so that someone was always designated to clean up after poker or pizza night. Even when it was his turn, Alex was glad to know that he wouldn't wake up to chaos and dirty dishes in the morning. Of course, none of these plans worked perfectly every time and the anxiety didn't go away completely. We worked on seeing each situation that went sideways as an opportunity to practice re-focusing on what he had control over. Each time he did that his obsessions about staying home and worries about getting sick diminished. As he found more success in his work and social routines, those related anxieties decreased, so his unhelpful habits of isolating and micromanaging the apartment diminished, which further improved his relationships with his roommates.

**Now You Try It!** Take a moment and think about the things that are stressing you out right now and make a list of them: Your stress list! Then make a list of the things that make you feel happy, calm, or at least not stressed; Your positive list! As you look at your twin lists, see if you notice the role that feeling in control plays with your emotional reactions to each list. For both lists, it may help to start out with small items that are going on today and then build up to the "big ticket items" that seem to trip you up time and again. Try not to over-think this exercise, these lists are just to set the stage. Once you've done this exercise, put the lists away for now they may come in handy later.

| | Stress list | Soothing list |
|---|---|---|
| **Physical** | | |
| **Mental** | | |
| **Emotional** | | |
| **Spiritual** | | |
| **Familial** | | |
| **Social** | | |
| **Professional** | | |
| **Community** | | |

*Chapter 7*

# THE COPING PLAN

To help illustrate our next concept, please welcome Eliot, a 75-year old widower. He lived alone and had two children who lived about 1000 miles away in two different cities. Eliot worked as a project supervisor at the Department of Public Works for over 40 years. He felt like he grew up at the DPW because he had worked there so long, and he knew everything there was to know about his city. His colleagues were his local family and they helped him get through the loss of his wife and his children moving away. As he got older, he noticed getting around on the job sites and in and out of the big trucks was becoming harder and harder. He also started getting more push back from the Board of Supervisors because he couldn't keep on top of all the various project details the way he had in the past. After suffering a bad fall on one of the worksites the DPW Director made him go to his doctor to get checked out. An extensive work-up found that Eliot had Parkinson's disease, which explained why his thinking and mobility were changing. He could not fully understand, at the time, what the implications of this disease were for his career and independent lifestyle. He struggled with how to prepare for what was to come.

When we're facing a problem that feels too big or has not endpoint in sight, it helps to have a plan to make things better. Clearly there is no single plan that will guarantee successful coping in every situation, but the steps below can serve as a template for how to feel less stuck.

**Step One: Notice Something is Wrong.**

This first step may sound obvious, but while we are living day to day, it can be hard to take a step back and look at what is making our lives harder. Sometimes we can't pinpoint exactly what the problem is. Other times we know exactly what the problem is, but it can seem too big to do anything about. In either case, defining the actual barriers is a useful place to start.

Eliot initially had a hard time figuring out what was getting in his way. At first, he ignored the early signs of his Parkinson's disease (PD) because he didn't know what it was. He knew he often didn't feel well that he was clumsier and more forgetful than he had been in the past, but the symptoms came on slowly and weren't consistent day to day. He could ignore the slow onset of PD because he could find reasons for each of the symptoms: He was tired because he had stayed up too late last night. His hands were shaky because he had too much coffee in the morning to help him wake up. He tripped on the trash laying around his work site because the new hires hadn't finished sweeping up. He had to admit after a while, however, that the pattern of his difficulties was not getting better. His friends at work were noticing as well but it took their encouragement, and his director's insistence, to go get checked out. He was reluctant and nervous to hear what the doctor was going to say. Once he heard the diagnosis, he began to understand his difficulties and he felt a weird sense of relief because his problems now made sense.

The basic problem was that Eliot's body and mind were not working as well as they had in the past. Until he went to the doctor, he couldn't see how all the symptoms related to each other. Once he understood what the core problem was, he was better able to address it. He went to community education groups with other patients to learn more about how PD was going to affect his life going forward. He worked hard to shift his perspective from taking his health for granted to learning how to manage a chronic illness with a lot of unknowns in the future. That shift in perspective opened him up to a lot of support and information that helped him feel less "crazy" and alone and prepared him to start thinking about what he wanted to do about it.

**Step Two: Set Short-Term Goals.**

Stress arises when we have no plan. This is true for all situations, but it's even more true for difficult situations. Goals can always change but to make forward progress, we need a sense of what's possible and what we're working toward. In general, goals are more likely to be met if they're realistic, achievable, and observable. "Realistic" means that the goal is within the realm of possibility, "achievable" means that you'll be able to get there if you work at it, and "observable" means that other people could see that you are making progress toward the goal.

Eliot's first goals were "I don't want to die" and "I don't want to be a burden on my kids." He felt strongly about both goals, and he wasn't wrong to start there. Those goals were so broad, however, that he wasn't going to have much control over making them come true. For example, "I don't want to die" isn't realistic, achievable, or observable. PD isn't a death sentence, for one thing, and he wasn't at risk for dying right away anyway, but in the long run he also wasn't immortal. When faced with an unrealistic goal, the solution is not to abandon it but rather revise it so that it can be more achievable. So, what was an observable goal that took "not dying" and reframed it with a more positive aim? Eliot needed to flip the goal, to focus more on how to live rather than how to "not die." Focusing on living with PD led to more specific actions that he could focus on, like "I want to stay healthy." This goal led to the doctors' visits, physical therapy, nutrition consults, and coping skills therapy, of course.

These were all ways to achieve the goal of living that were within his reach because they were easily definable, observable, and realistic.

His second goal, "I don't want to be a burden," seemed a little clearer, but still did not lead to an obvious plan of action. His children didn't know how to help him feel like less of a burden when they talked on the phone. He had been so independent all his life, it was hard for them to conceive of him as anything else. It wasn't clear what his needs were going to be over time and there was only so much his kids could do since they weren't local. Eliot learned, through our work together, that he was going to feel more successful if his goals had action items. We worked on refining this goal by adding "I won't be a burden **if I get my plans in order now**." That became a stronger goal once it was further defined as "I won't be a burden if **I get a power of attorney and health-care proxy and talk to a lawyer about setting up my will**." It became stronger still once it had the added clarity of "I won't be a burden if **I set up my power of attorney with my son David and health-care proxy with my niece Tammy, and since she lives locally, she can introduce me to her lawyer who can set up my will**." As each version of the goal got clearer, Eliot became less worried about what to do next. The first version of the goal: "I don't want to be a burden" was a good starting point, but the last version was much more realistic, with its clear directions. Once he had steps to follow and specific people to reach out to, it was easier for Eliot to talk with his children about what he needed. His children felt better knowing they could help him achieve his goals. Eliot felt better knowing he had more control; both over how he approached the process and how he followed through. To make success even more likely, he started the habit of writing his goals down and then working on rephrasing them step by step, getting as specific as possible until he had clear paths to follow.

**Step Three: Find the Barriers.**

In the process of defining, refining, and working toward our goals, it's inevitable to run into barriers. Barriers are anything that interferes with us coping with the challenges we face. The only goals with no barriers are the ones we have already finished (or the ones we're doing right this minute). We should give ourselves some credit for getting those tasks done, but they don't tend to be the goals we worry about.

Barriers can arise from sources inside, or outside, of us. Inside barriers can be physical, mental, or emotional challenges. Some are short term and others are part of our core make up. Outside barriers can be anything, including other people, the system, or events going on around us. They can be people not understanding our limitations or capacities. The system may not be set up for equal access to resources or doesn't treat people of different backgrounds the same. Maybe not enough time has passed, or we have been distracted by other things. When we discover a barrier, two common, but unhelpful, reaction strategies can happen. We either try to ignore it or we focus on it too much. We try to ignore things that we hope will just go away on their own, like physical symptoms or awkward relationships at work. This can be effective over the short run, but long term the barrier still exists, even if we don't want to deal with it. We get overly focused on barriers when we believe that, if we can just figure it out, we can stop it from happening. Focusing only on the problem, however, magnifies its power and robs us of the chance to find alternative solutions.

A healthier strategy is to look at the barriers honestly, and see them for what they are, nothing more than the thing between us and our goals. We don't need to get stuck on how many there are, or what types they are, but rather focus on how we are going to get past them. When Eliot first learned about his diagnosis, he didn't know what he didn't know. He didn't have a lawyer and wasn't familiar with legal forms, like a health care proxy, since he had never needed them before. He didn't know who to ask for consultation, or how to start toward his goal of "not being a burden." He realized he had to take "a hard look" at what he needed to learn and "swallow" his pride to ask for help.

Eliot discovered that he had a range of internal and external barriers. His physical barriers came from the variation, and progressive deterioration, of his muscle strength and energy over time. Some days were harder than others for getting around and making all his medical appointments. He had a mental barrier due to his lack of knowledge about what medical and legal paperwork he needed. His emotional barriers came from the fear and sadness he felt as he tried to anticipate what the course of his disease would be like, and the impact that would have on his family and friends. The external barriers related to the physical and mental requirements of his job that could only be accommodated to a certain extent. He had to face how other people reacted to him, especially if they did not understand PD. Some people thought he was drunk when he had trouble walking or mentally unfit when his speech was labored and slow. No matter the source or the type of barrier, Eliot knew that any one of them could derail him if he allowed it. He knew that he couldn't ignore any of them, at the same time he couldn't get stuck on any one of them either.

Feeling stuck often happens when we first face a crisis because the barriers can seem insurmountable. Coping is the art of finding paths around our barriers. Defining his barrier as "I don't want to be a burden" started Eliot on the path to overcome it. Naming it allowed him to know what he didn't want, so he could talk with friends to find out how they approached similar problems. Once he had his friend's support and advice, he felt strong enough to call his children to tell them what was going on. As he talked with them about what to do next they helped him figure out what the necessary paperwork would be and the types of professionals that could be helpful to him in various ways. Having the professionals' support and advice helped him make plans that gave him back a sense of control and helped him feel like less of a burden. He felt safe knowing that his wishes were clear and would be honored. Eliot summed it up best: "When I look at problems, that's all I see; when I look at solutions, that's all I see." Fighting the urge to either ignore, or get overwhelmed by, the barriers in our lives can be key to successful coping. Only when we understand what our barriers are, can we make plans to overcome them.

**Step Four: Focus on Your Strengths.**

So now that we know where we're going and can see what's getting in our way, how do we accomplish our goals? Step 4 helps us define the strengths we'll need to overcome our barriers.

In much the same way that barriers can be internal or external, so too can our strengths and assets. Internal assets can be our literal physical abilities (like muscle strength, speed, or balance) or our mental capacities (like wit, intellect, or memory for names) or even our emotional capacity (like compassion, empathy, or sense of humor). We tend to think about the tangible assets, like physical strength, more often since that's what people see from the outside. It is our intangible assets, however, such as our faith, work ethic, and social skills, that frequently determine how well we are coping. No matter what the specific type or category of strength, we all have some of them. They are inside us already and we don't need to change anything or learn anything new to access them. External strengths are things we have around us, not inside us. These are things like supportive family and friends, access to good jobs, healthy environment, and a safe and just society. These are also critical components to our coping, but they are not so evenly distributed in our world. Eliot was an only child and not born into a family of privilege. He didn't earn a huge salary at the DPW so he couldn't rely on those types of assets to get by. He knew he could rely on his family for some things but, like many of us, he relied on his "family of choice" friend group to support him most of the time. Sometimes that support was in person and sometimes it was virtual, like with on-line support communities. These external assets often will look very different from region to region, culture to culture, or group to group. Nevertheless, it is important for each of us to look for the people, places, and things around us that can support our healthy coping.

Another nice feature is that we can use strengths from one area of our life to help us overcome barriers from some other area. Eliot, for example, overcame his physical barrier of reduced balance and stamina by using his strong social skills to ask friends for rides to appointments. He overcame his knowledge barrier about important legal issues by using his work ethic to get, and understand, the necessary information. He overcame his emotional barrier of worrying about burdening his children by using his trust in them when he asked for help. Once Eliot decided what was getting in his way, he was free to use any of his strengths to overcome the barriers, sometimes in conventional ways like going to the gym to get stronger, as well as in new ways, like using his social skills to get vital information.

The other good news about strengths is that we can always build new ones, adding to the ones we already have. Eliot, for example, learned how to do breathing relaxation exercises to help him calm down during times of high stress. He learned that information about his illness was not so scary once he learned how to use it to his advantage. He got a lot of details from his online support groups that allowed him to ask better questions to his doctors. He learned how to be more physically efficient, like getting up and out early, since he had more energy in the morning and before the heat of the day. If needed, he took a nap in the afternoon when he was feeling drawn down, which allowed him to be re-energized in the evening so he could still spend time with his friends, whose support was critical to his positive outlook. He learned to cope with strangers who misunderstood why he walked or talked like he did by giving them a "mini-lecture" on Parkinson's disease that he mixed with his sense of humor, ("I give them a piece of my mind, but not too big a piece since I don't have much to spare!"). New strengths like these are skills, and learning a new skill always takes practice, time, and effort. When Eliot sometimes struggled with mastering a new skill, he went back to his best asset-- being social--and then worked his way up from there.

**Step Five: Putting it All Together.**

Eliot put together his coping plan by taking stock of each of its pieces. Initially, the Parkinson's diagnosis left him feeling fragmented and unsure of how to move forward. He was quick to come up with his goals of "not dying" and "not being a burden", but then realized that some goals were achievable, while others weren't. The process of thinking through his goals helped him weed out the likely from the unlikely, but in the beginning, it was hard to tell them apart. Lots of goals seem out of reach until we look at the specific challenges that stand in our way. Eliot was initially overwhelmed with all the barriers he faced. He focused on how his physical abilities were changing, the internal barriers of not knowing what questions to ask, the external barriers of other people not giving him the support that he needed. Eliot had to learn how to overcome the former and react better to the latter. He had some ideas about what his strengths were, but they seemed like a separate issue, unconnected to his challenges. He knew he had a solid group of friends and his kids loved him, even from afar, but that did not seem relevant to managing his disease. Taking a step back, to look at how each part of the solution-seeking process worked together, allowed him to see answers where none existed before. Each time he defined and refined his goals, they became easier to aim at. Going through this routine underscored his core belief of being independent, even if that meant getting help from others to overcome a certain challenge. He realized that taking a hard look at what was not going well allowed him to shift his thinking about limits, from barriers to targets of opportunity. Each time he chose strengths to overcome a barrier, helping him achieve a goal, he gained confidence in himself. Over time this became the new standard for how he navigated his life, allowing him to achieve goals he never thought possible!

**Now You Try It!** When you do this, use a form like this next one to write down goals that you want to achieve in the upcoming week, month, 6 months, and a year. The table has 4 columns: Goals, Barriers, Strengths, and Next Steps because seeing the problem in a more visual way can help you develop an action plan. I encourage you to try it with a variety of goals, some you are already planning on doing and some that may be "reach" goals. Picking goals with different timelines can help you practice thinking about what goals are more likely to be achieved, as well as which ones will require more patience and dedication over a longer time frame. Try to remember to go back to this sheet regularly over the next few weeks and months to check in on how you are progressing toward the goals you set out. If you are on track, awesome! If you are not, review, revise, and reengage!

| Time | Goal | Barrier | Strength | Next Step |
|---|---|---|---|---|
| Week | | | | |
| 1 Month | | | | |
| 6 Month | | | | |
| 1 Year | | | | |

*Chapter 8*

# THE TOOLBOX

Building on "the diamond" concept, from Chapter 3, that our sense of self is based on the full collection of our facets, "the toolbox" concept focuses on recognizing skills we already have, as well as building new ones, to use with our various facets. There's an old joke that if all you have is a hammer, everything looks like a nail. Building the variety and number of tools in our toolbox broadens the range of things we can do and expands our capacity to do them. Just ask any skilled worker, be it a carpenter or a neurosurgeon; having the right tools is key to success.

We all develop tools for coping with life's challenges over time. We learn our first coping strategies as children and then continue to refine those tools as we get older and gain new knowledge and abilities. Over time we develop a core set of skills that we use most often and discard ones that don't work so well for us. But there are times when something unforeseen happens and our "go-to" tools aren't up to the task or we discover that we don't have the right tools at all. Darlene found this out with her job disruption. She was confronted with the choice of staying with her company and moving far from home or staying in her hometown where her supports were and changing jobs late in her career. Prior to this challenging time in her life, her core set of coping tools included her work ethic, exercising to manage the stresses of everyday life, and downtime with friends to recharge. She had other skills as well, but these habits were her most effective. They allowed her to be successful at her job, stay physically healthy, and feel supported while she navigated the various currents in her life. When the work crisis hit, Darlene's usual routines weren't enough. She suddenly had so much work to do that her normal work habits could not keep up with all the tasks on her plate. Going to the gym on top of all that extra work only added to her stress. Getting so caught up in the big decision further undercut her availability to her colleagues and friends when she needed them the most.

The problem was not with her old "tools" as they were still effective, but they were not up to the more intense demands of the crisis. She needed to add some new tools to her toolbox. Through her therapy sessions, Darlene learned new work skills like putting her schedule on the shared calendar, so her colleagues knew when she was, and wasn't, available and becoming more assertive to clarify expectations with them. She also worked on re-setting her own expectations by prioritizing her health to be as important as her work projects. She learned that she worked better when she set aside time for breaks, so she set a clear agenda which helped her stick to a schedule. She used those breaks to get in "mini" sessions of exercise, like walking the stairs at the office or going to a yoga class before work started. She also used the breaks to check in on her friends and family, via video chat or phone so she could still feel connected. She took Sunday's off as her day of rest and rejuvenation as well, which helped her prepare for the upcoming week. Once the initial crisis passed, Darlene went back to using her regular coping tools most of the time, but she also had the new tools available to add into the "mix." Recognizing that she had the capacity to pick up new coping tools, when she needed them the most, boosted her confidence as she moved forward. That confidence turned out to be a new and very positive tool in and of itself, because she felt more in control when faced with new stressful situations.

An additional concept that Darlene found useful was getting rid of tools that did not work so well. Since we start accumulating them as children, some tools are going to serve us better than others. Our tried-and-true tools are always going to be useful, but sometimes we keep tools that are "broken" or may just be outdated. Using alcohol to cope with our disappointments, for example, is like a broken wrench that doesn't get the job done and only leaves us with bloody knuckles in the end. Bursting into tears is a more acceptable way to express frustration as a toddler than it is for a bank manager. Although, it can still be helpful as a release, once you are home from work and have time to yourself, or are surrounded by nonjudgy friends or family. These tools will not help you and may even hurt you, by making matters worse. Some tools are rarely if ever used but still have utility when needed, like angrily fighting back if you're getting mugged. Sometimes the issue is different tools for different situations, like sometimes you need a sledgehammer (literally fighting back) and sometimes you need an upholstery hammer (pointing out a microaggression). This is not an all or nothing process, but it's useful to take stock of the tools that you have and decide which ones are still useful and which ones are not. Getting rid of tools that don't work also makes more room to acquire new tools that work better. Darlene realized her toolbox worked better, and made the crisis more manageable, when she let go of the idea that she had to control everything at work and at home and instead added healthy expectations and assertiveness. Our coping is improved when we find new positive ways to respond to our stress and stop relying on old habits (outdated coping tools) that no longer serve their purpose. Sometimes we can do this on our own and sometimes it helps to talk with friends or professionals, to get a fresh perspective on techniques we have not thought about. Either way, having, and using, the right coping tool for the job is something you have control over and the more tools you have, the more tasks you can master.

**Now You Try it!** Take stock of the tools you are already using to cope with stress. What tools are working well for you? What tools are "broken" and end up causing more harm than good? Remember that old tools may work perfectly fine so you don't need to re-invent the wheel all the time, but it can be helpful to do an inventory of the current ones so that you can begin to see what, if any, new ones would be useful.

| **My Toolbox** | | What I have works well | What I have seems broken | What I need to do the job better |
|---|---|---|---|---|
| Internal Tools and Assets | Physical | | | |
| | Mental | | | |
| | Emotional | | | |
| | Spiritual | | | |
| External Tools and Assets | Familial | | | |
| | Social | | | |
| | Professional | | | |
| | Community | | | |

*Chapter 9*

# THE THREE BOXES

This concept is brought to you with the help of Samantha. Samantha was a 55-year-old woman living with her partner Jessica in an old mill town, working as a supervisor on the production floor for one of the timber companies. Due to slowdowns in demand, and stiff foreign competition, the company had massive layoffs and then eventually closed. Samantha loved her location and lifestyle and access to the forests and lakes. She liked her job as well but once it was gone there weren't too many other jobs, at her level, in the area. The timber mill's closing had an impact over the whole region. Jessica, worked in one of the downtown breweries so they could stay afloat, but just barely. Finding a job that matched Samantha's qualifications meant they were going to have to make some hard choices.

Many of us have worked in jobs where the items on our to-do list seem never ending. Like coming back from a vacation to see that list of work-orders or emails stuffing our in-boxes. It can be hard, and time consuming, to wade through it all, separating out the important issues from the unimportant, and we can miss the essential messages or get distracted by irrelevant ones. This can happen in our non-working lives as well. "Stuff happens" and we get too much on our plate and, as the old saying goes, "when it rains it pours." When stressful events start to pile up, it can be hard to decide what to do first. In the abstract we know some things are more important than others, but if we only have one "in-box," then it can be hard to sort out the things we have control over versus the things we don't. The Three Boxes technique is a method that helps us focus on doing just that.

**Box #1**: "I definitely have control over this." This is the box for all the things we currently do every day. We have all the resources, the energy, the ability, the time, and basically anything else we need to get the job done. This can range from the basic: "What am I going to wear today?" or "What am I going to have for breakfast?" to the more involved: "Today I'm presenting the project that I know inside and out and I'm so ready!" or "I have my follow-up appointment with Dr. Jones today. I sent her my questions already; she knows my concerns and I booked a full hour to make sure I get my answers!"

Most of the time we don't have any trouble managing the items in Box #1, but it is worth mentioning because we often take them for granted. When we are under a lot of stress it's easy to forget that our lives still go on, and that we're meeting our daily obligations, often despite the mess going on around us. If we think about it at all, we tend to diminish these activities because we think they're nothing special: "Of course I'm doing that, duh! Doesn't everyone do that? Why make such a big deal out of something so basic?!" The answer is because we all can feel paralyzed when facing a crisis. Box # 1 is there to remind us that we are not helpless in all aspects of our lives, and recognizing that, is a step in the right direction. It is also true that these things would not have gotten done without us and taking credit for even small victories opens the door to the bigger victories to come.

When Samantha first learned about her impending lay-off from the timber mill, she was totally stressed about what she and Jessica were going to do. There were so many decisions to make about what to do next: where to work, where to live, how they were going to pay the bills. At first, Samantha felt like her whole life was just one big pile of "stuff." Trying to face all the different issues at the same time made it hard to feel successful managing any of them. She didn't give herself credit for all the things she was doing every day because she was distracted by all the things that she was not doing. Like many of us, she tended to focus on the areas where she came up short since that was where her emotional energy was going. Once she took the time to acknowledge what she was getting done every day, it was harder to feel so helpless and overwhelmed. Samantha's Box #1 successes included things like giving her full effort at her part-time jobs and calling some of the headhunters she met at a conference the year before. She started talking to friends and family, and even prior competitors--anyone who might know of an opening or job prospect she could investigate. At the end of the day, she could take stock of all the things she had done--from the basic to the complex--and feel a little less lost. Although she didn't find a job or fix her financial problems every day, Samantha validated for herself that she was not powerless or passive in the face of her career set-back.

**Box #2:** "<u>I will have control over this</u>." This is the box for all the things that we will be able to manage, at some point, just not today. Today we are missing some crucial element; like it's not time yet, or we don't have the energy, resources, or knowledge to complete the job, and we won't be able to fix it until we get that missing piece. To be clear this is not so much an issue of <u>if</u> we'll get it done, but <u>when</u>. It might happen tomorrow, or months from now, but eventually we will get what we need, the item will move into Box #1, and we'll take care of it. The passage of time always plays a role in Box # 2, but often we need to work toward our goals in other ways as well; by working on healing or learning a new skill or getting more information. In Samantha's case, making appointments and searching for the right job opportunity had many aspects in Box #2. As with Box #1 items, she had some general ideas of what needed to be done, but she could see that none of them were going to happen today. Box #2 issues can also range from the mundane to the complex. "Looks like we'll have time to do laundry on Sunday" or "Maybe if we save our money, we can still take some time off next spring" or "If I learn how to weld, I can apply for that job at the garage." No matter how much she wanted to get it done, it was not going to happen until she had the missing piece (time had passed, she'd saved the money, or learned the skills). As soon as she got what she needed, the task shifted from Box #2 to Box #1 and she took care of it, just like all the other Box #1 items that day.

At the end of the day there will always be things in Box #2. That's the way it's supposed to be. Samantha found making an actual master to-do list, full of all the things she had to get done, very useful. She posted it next to her calendar and used it as a place to jot down all the things she was planning; for later today, later this week, or some other time in the future. Samantha sorted the tasks that she was already getting done into Box #1. Then she sorted the ones that were pending into Box #2. If there were no other job-related tasks to do, she distracted herself by going to the gym and working off some of that extra emotional energy. Her house was spotless! She felt less stressed about all the things in Box #2 as she saw them getting done, over time. That master list became a working document where she sorted out what the next days, weeks, and months were going to look like. This list not only helped her manage her job hunt, but once she got her new job, it helped her manage the many deadlines, on the multiple projects, that became her responsibility. She loved seeing each item shift out of Box #2 and join the growing list of Box #1 accomplishments.

**Box #3**: "I will never have control over this." This can be the hardest box of all. Box #3 holds all the things we didn't have, don't have, and never will have, any control over. As with the prior two boxes, items in this box range from the basic issues that affect everyone, like the weather or traffic, to the more complex and personal, like coping with cancer, losing money in the stock market or casino, having our factory jobs moved overseas or given to robots. Box #3 is where most of our frustrations live because it holds all the things we want to have control over, but don't. We feel our greatest stress when we are rummaging around in Box #3, wishing we could change what happened in the past or know what's going to happen in the future. This is where we look for rational explanations for things that have none.

Samantha was challenged by this box as well. Her initial reaction to losing her job focused a lot on "Why me?" and "What could I have done differently?" She spent a lot of time at first looking over her past job evaluations and the company newsletters trying to figure out what she might have missed about her work performance or the direction the company was taking. When she wasn't looking for a new job, she read up on the issues affecting her industry to try to understand what led to the mill closing. She learned about trade policy and how little timber industry workers overseas are paid and how those companies can charge less for their products. In the end she came to see that her job, her company, and her town were only one small part of a much larger economic story. Her timber mill closing didn't seem as personal once she learned about the dismal conditions in timber mills overseas. It didn't change her reality, of course, because she still lost her job, but she stopped spending as much energy and time being angry. She stopped asking the question, "Why did this happen to me?" and started asking the question, "What am I going to do about it?" Her answers lay in Box #1 and Box #2!

Before Samantha went to sleep at the end of the day, she started a habit of reviewing her 3 Boxes. She felt good looking at her list from Box #1 with all the items crossed off, reminding herself that she was not helpless or stuck. Box #2 was her on-going, to-do list, with all the items she knew she would be accomplishing in the days and weeks ahead. Normally, this box would have caused a lot of anxiety, but it became the place where she kept track of her plans and described the steps she would be taking on her life journey. Having a full to-do list was a good thing because it underscored what she would be accomplishing next. At the same time, she knew she didn't have to worry about any of it that day because those were all future items. Box #3 came to be known as her "trash can" since there was nothing valuable in it. Samantha imagined Box #3 had a plastic bag liner in it that she would take out every night, with the rest of the garbage in her life.

This was especially helpful when people tried to be supportive by telling her that she would be fine and that she should stop worrying about everything all the time. The idea that she should just be calm in the face of such a career disruption seemed crazy at first, until she recognized that she was already handling everything in Box #1 without any worry. She similarly grew to feel confident that she would be able to handle everything in Box #2, eventually, when the situation was right. Finally she realized that she could stop worrying about the rest of the stuff in Box #3 because she never had any control over that stuff anyway. She also came to see that the very act of sorting her worries was something she had control over, allowing her to use her emotional energy in the best way possible.

**Now You Try It!** Start with a problem you already know how to figure out and sort its parts into the 3 Boxes. For example, "What am I going to eat for dinner tomorrow?" is a problem you know how to fix. Once you see how the process works in a simple way, try it with an actual problem you are trying to face up to. In the beginning, you will find that a lot of stuff goes into Box #2 because the to-do list is big in the beginning. As things get done you will see more clearly what you can fix and what you can let go of.

| **Problem** | **BOX # 1**<br>I have total control right now | **BOX # 2**<br>I will have control in the future | **BOX # 3**<br>I will never have control |
|---|---|---|---|
| | | | |
| | | | |
| | | | |

*Chapter 10*

# THE FIVE PART QUESTION

Eliot faced a major challenge of how to manage a disease that was going to gradually take away control in his life. He had always been in good control of his actions and decisions, so the idea of losing his physical and mental abilities not only terrified him but made him feel helpless. Having read this far in the book you know that control is key to coping well with stress but unfortunately situations like Eliots make it hard to feel in control. Eliot had the common reaction of getting swept up into an escalating spiral of worry. Not knowing what to do magnified the feeling of being out of control, which made the stress even worse. Eliot knew he had to find a way out of that spiral so he could figure out a way forward. In his counseling sessions, Eliot found great comfort in having a guiding principle as a first step in regaining control. That guiding principle is embodied in the following 5 Part Question:

**"Am I doing the best I can with what I've got right now to make the most out of today?"**

The first part of the question, "**Am I doing**" is there to remind us that we are in charge of how we are "doing" our lives. We are in charge of what we do and what we don't do. Eliot found it helpful to remember that he had always been, still was, and would continue to be, the one deciding what he did with his life. It was a core value of Eliot's to be in charge of his own actions and decisions and he was reassured that aspect of his life had not changed. At first, however, the idea of being in control of the day-to-day tasks did not seem like groundbreaking news. Eliot, like most people, never gave much thought to all the decisions he made each day. Small tasks--such as getting out of bed, getting dressed, paying the bills, and tidying up the house, or calling his friends -- are easy to ignore because we do them without a lot of thought and they don't carry as much weight as big decisions do. Eliot came to realize, however, that these admittedly minor tasks were the foundation that kept his finances stable, his house orderly, and his friends engaged in his life. That day-to-day stability then allowed him to do the more major things, like get the medical care he needed or make decisions about his work schedule. Recognizing that even small tasks, like where he ate dinner or what he watched on TV, were important, helped Eliot see that he had some control over how he lived his life and helped him feel less helpless in the face of all his medical decisions. These were Eliot's Box #1 items.

The second part of the question, "**the best I can**" underscores another of Eliot's core values. He had always tried to do the best he could with the skills he'd had in life and that part of him had not changed either. He was fond of pointing out that he was never a "slacker" like some of the other guys at the DPW yard! Early in the diagnostic process, Eliot second guessed some of his prior life choices since things had not turned out the way he had wanted them to. He worried that maybe he did something wrong in the past that led to him getting Parkinson's Disease. It was tempting to judge his past efforts based on how things were turning out in the present. Personal factors, like effort, certainly can contribute to how some things turn out for us, but Parkinson's has so many other biological aspects that shape long-term outcomes, personal effort can't be considered a cause of it. Clearly, no one starts out a project, or approaches a challenging life event, saying, "I'm going to give this a half-baked effort" or "I'll do this, but I am not going to try very hard." When Eliot reassessed his life, based on the effort he put in along the way, rather than the outcomes he was facing, he felt more successful. He could see that, when he had put his energy into things he had control over, he had done the best he could. When he had focused on the things outside of his control, he had felt more helpless. He was less pessimistic about his future when he realized that he still had responsibility for his effort, and he knew his work ethic was not going to disappear just because he got Parkinson's Disease.

These first two parts of the question, (1) Am I doing, (2) the best I can, are there to help us remember our core strengths. Core strengths tend to be set early on in life and to be consistent over time. We all fall back on these core principles when faced with life's challenges. Eliot initially felt like his world had been turned upside down when he found out about the Parkinson's diagnosis. He knew that the progressively debilitating disease, would ultimately stop him from living his life as he always had. He felt overwhelmed thinking about the many areas of his routine that were going to change, like learning new diet and exercise habits, as well as new medications and medical providers. All of that was unfamiliar and scary until he took a step back and realized that the bedrock of his personality, that had carried him this far, was not going to change. He felt less helpless as he came to see that his strengths, honed over a long career, and close relationships with his family and friends, were still a part of him. He may have been a "newbie" in the world of Parkinson's Disease, but he was an "old-hand" at the skills of coping with life's challenges.

The third part of the question, "**with what I've got**" does change over time. In contrast to the first two parts of the question, what you've "got" in life is not nearly as stable. This refers to the energy we use to face life's challenges. We can also see it reflected by changes in our strength, our finances, our health, our social or family support. It can change slowly and naturally over the course of our lives, as we age, or it can change over the course of weeks or days or even minutes, if we get a bad diagnosis, lose a job, or have an accident. No matter how fast the change comes, however, it alters how we see the world. Recognizing that our energy is not a constant, helps us manage our expectations more effectively. Eliot, for example, had known he was having more trouble walking for a while, but had always come up with reasons to explain it away, like being tired or having leg cramps because he wasn't eating enough bananas. These explanations helped him avoid having to face the reality of his deteriorating health, but when he finally heard the Parkinson's diagnosis, it still took his breath away and he felt like the floor "opened up" beneath him. At first, all he could think about were the difficult parts of living with a progressive disease; physically, mentally, and emotionally. After a while, he could see that it wasn't all bad, of course, because having the diagnosis helped him understand his symptoms, so they weren't such a mystery. He could also see that some days were better than others. Knowing his diagnosis didn't change how his current life was going, but once he knew about the long-term changes, he could never go back to thinking about life the way he used to.

The variability of the "what I've got" part is central to this guiding principle because it underscores the importance of adjusting our expectations as we go along. As is true in health, in business, or any other part of our lives; flexibility is key to healthy coping. Many people don't want to talk about the idea that life sometimes sucks because it feels like we're inviting it to happen. This guiding principle allows us to consider the fact that whether life is a bummer or a hoot; we can use our energy level to set our expectations appropriately and reasonably. But setting expectations requires us to have some reference point and how we pick that point can make all the difference.

Finding that point of comparison can be very difficult. We can't know how we compare to the future since we're not there yet and other instances from the present aren't different enough. Sometimes we compare ourselves to a professional athlete or movie star or internet influencer, which also isn't fair because most of us never had those talents to begin with. Sometimes we compare ourselves to someone we know who hasn't had a crisis yet, so their life seems better also. Most of us compare our present self to an earlier version because that feels more realistic, but it still doesn't do justice to all that we've gone through in life. I joke with my clients that I'd probably pick when I was 35 years old because I remember feeling pretty good about myself back then (please don't ask my family!). During the early days after his diagnosis Eliot felt frustrated, thinking "This is so hard, why can't I handle this like I have handled other things?" Eliot was comparing himself to a past capacity that, to his credit, was real at the time, but wasn't helpful now. The comparison couldn't help him reclaim those past capacities now and it didn't consider all that he had been through in the intervening years.

At the same time, recognizing that he was not at that earlier "high point" was not the same as giving up or accepting defeat. Just because he didn't have 100% of his former energy didn't mean he was left with 0%. Like all of us, Eliot's normal energy ebbed and flowed over the day, the week, as well as over the course of his treatment for Parkinson's. Most of us don't pay close attention to the energy in our bodies. We generally know how we feel when we are tired or awake but don't pay much attention to the shades of grey in between. When we can tune into to the energy in our bodies, we can set more realistic expectations for ourselves.

When Eliot started to pay attention to how much energy he felt in his body at different times of the day, and on different days, he learned how to "right-size" what he expected of himself. When he was feeling 80% of his "normal" energy, he would expect himself to give 80%. When he felt at 50%, his goal for that time or day was the full 50%. There were times when he felt like he only had 20% to give, so he set his goals with that in mind. For Eliot, an 80% day felt just like a normal day; he could do all the chores and tasks that he would normally take on. A 50% day was more focused on getting some things done around the home, but scaling back going out in public, with all the traffic and hustle and bustle. A 20% day was basically having an instant "cup-a-soup" watching movies, under a blanket, on the couch. In each case, no matter how he felt, Eliot was still giving his best effort based on the energy he had at that moment in the day. Readjusting his expectations, based on his energy level, led to a lot less disappointment because he was keeping to his core values of "doing" tasks "the best he could."

Eliot found "expectation management" helpful when he talked with other people about how he was coping as well. Well-meaning people would ask him how he was doing, sometimes with a casual greeting like "Hey, how's it going?" and sometimes in a more pointed way like "Is your Parkinson's getting tough for you yet?" He faced it at work, even though he was only there part-time, and sometimes completely randomly at the grocery store or in his neighborhood. No matter what the other person's intent, it was often hard to know what the right answer should be. One option was to say everything was "fine" even though often that was not completely true. The other option was to "tell the whole truth and nothing but the truth" with all the daily details of his health and medical treatments. This took a lot of time, really was no one's business, and most people didn't want to hear it anyway. Since his children were out of state, they had no way of knowing how he was doing on a day-to-day basis, so it was a frequent conversation with them, but even they found it hard to know how to respond. They wanted to focus on solutions but were unable to know how much or what kind of help he needed, frustrating them all. Like many people in this situation, Eliot started to not answer the phone and often preferred staying home by himself. The "0 to 100" scale was a useful shorthand for answering these questions since it allowed him to rank how he was doing in a way most people understood. He might say, "well I'm at 75% today-- so not too bad, just working on my projects!" Most people understood that when he said he was at 75-85%, he didn't need much help. He learned he could ask for help with certain tasks if he was between 45% and 75%, and people responded more appropriately since it was clearer what level of support he needed. If he had things to do when he was between 25% and 45% it was clear he would need help, or just postpone that task and rest, with no expectations of getting anything done that day. When the percentage changed over the course of the day, he could adjust what he told people accordingly. In response to someone asking to visit with him, he could say, "Yes please come over, I'm a good 75% right now, but if I feel like I am slipping below 40%, I'm going to ask you to go home." This was not only a clear and brief way of telling people what he felt up to doing, it also made it easier to accept the help others offered. Eliot came to see himself as the "international expert" on how much energy he had, as well as how much, and what kind of, support or assistance he needed. No one in the world knew what he felt like better than him.

The fourth part of the question "**right now**" helps us focus on the present. When Eliot was unhappy with his current life situation, he noticed that his thoughts would often wander off to either the past or the future. But, like most of us, he felt sadder when he thought about the past because he knew he couldn't go back to re-live the happier times or change what had already happened. After the diagnosis he tended to dwell on how much he had changed over time. When his thoughts wandered off to the future, he felt more worried because he couldn't know what was going to happen next. How was he going to manage when his problems got worse? What if something else went wrong? He couldn't prepare for things that hadn't happened yet, and the list of potential troubles seemed endless. At the same time, when people told Eliot to "keep it in today" he knew that was no recipe for feeling consistently happy either. The day-to-day challenges were the ones that got him in to the doctors and diagnosed in the first place. So, if he wasn't happy thinking about the past, or the future, and he wasn't always happy about what was going on "right now" either, what was the solution?

The solution comes in understanding that our emotions are reactions, not so much to the timeframe, as to how much control we have. The past is already done, and the future is yet to be determined, so we have no control over them at this moment. When we are upset about the present it is usually because we don't have control over what is happening now. We can see this pattern, on a small scale, in ourselves, when things don't go as we planned, and we can see it on a large scale in the civil unrest that happens in countries all over the world. People rebel when they feel they have no other way of getting control.

So, staying in the moment is not the goal because there is some magic there, but rather because that is the only time frame we have any chance of being in control. Now as Eliot found out, it may be popular to "stay in the moment" but it is not that easy. Clearly, none of us can live completely in the present all the time since we would never have groceries in the house or get to our appointments if we did. To clarify, the difference between planning and staying in the moment is between *thinking* and *doing*. We all need to think about the future, to be able to plan for it, but we only have actual control over what we do in the present. Spending too much time thinking about the future interferes with what we need to do right now, which can lead to our feeling helpless.

The other concept to consider is that the intensity of our negative emotions reflects how much control we feel we have in that moment. The stronger the intensity, the less control we feel, be it in the past, present, or future. The fact that emotions become more intense based on how much control we feel, however, means that they can act like a signal rather than a state of being we need to endure. As we talked about in Chapter 4, shifting our understanding of emotions to being more like a signal allows us to have more control over how we respond to circumstances. Many of us, like Eliot, think of our negative emotions as something we have no power to change, like a storm, or fog bank, that comes out of nowhere, settles in and surrounds us. When he understood that his emotional reactions signaled where his thoughts had gone (too far into the past or too far into the future) he could see a way to have more control. When he felt sad it was likely because he was thinking too much about the past and vice versa. Similarly with worry and thoughts about the future. Eliot thought of his emotional signals the same way he thought about the lights on his truck dashboard. They were there to alert him to potential problems so he could avoid difficulties down the road. When he noticed sadness, he worked to bring his thoughts back from the past. If he noticed anxiety, he tried to bring his thoughts back from the future. If we pay attention and respond appropriately to these signals, in the present, we will be better able to cope with our stress, much like our vehicle will run more smoothly if we pay attention to the "check engine" light.

The fifth and final part of the question: "**to make the most out of today**" sums up its core point. Taken by itself, it sounds suspiciously like many of the other messages we get in our daily lives. We should always be striving to achieve something, or we must get it done today because tomorrow will be too late. That drumbeat toward achieving things obviously has an upside when it helps us get things done, but it can easily morph into something unhealthy when it becomes an end in and of itself. The final aspect of the question sums up the goal of the principle, which is less about accumulating stuff and more about what we need mentally and emotionally. The notion of the "most" is more akin to living fully and how we benefit from this day. It is based on what we bring to the table and is relative to our own capacity rather than some external benchmark, like what our boss wants or some societal expectation. It emphasizes "today" not because tomorrow is too late but because it brings our goals within reach, to the only day we have any control. If we can make the most out of today, and then we do it again tomorrow, and the day after that, then we will be able to make the most out of our week, month, year, and hopefully our lives. We can't predict what our future will hold for us, but we can know that if we have made the most of every day leading up to it, we will have few regrets.

In summary, the 5 Part Question helps us look for near term goals that are realistic and achievable, understanding that circumstances can change and not everyone starts out in the same place. It reminds us that we're always in charge of ourselves, and that our inner strengths and bed-rock capacities will keep us stable in times of crisis. It can help us re-set our expectations, both for ourselves, as well as those around us, so that we can react in healthier ways to what we are going through. It uses our emotions to keep our focus on the present, reminding us that we don't have to change the past, or predict the future, to be able to live life fully. The 5 Part question serves as a guiding principle because answering "yes", as we do most of the time, is a way to reaffirm we are on the right track. On the rare occasion that we answer "no" it is an opportunity for us to take stock of where we are missing the mark and allows us to get back on track toward making life better. Eliot used this guiding principle to reclaim control over how he was managing his life. He focused on doing his exercises and taking his medications every day and staying connected with his friends and family. He was better able to talk about his situation and only ask for the help that he needed so he could remain independent. He worked to make the most of the time he had so that he would not have regrets about how he faced his challenges as he got older. He knew that no matter how much energy he had, or lost, due to the Parkinson's disease, he had the power to live each day, good or bad, to its fullest--something no one and no disease could take away from him. He liked to say, "if I live to be 100 or I get abducted by aliens next Thursday, my life is going to be full!"

In Summary:

| | | |
|---|---|---|
| **Am I doing** | you are still the one in charge of what you are doing | same as always |
| **The Best I Can** | your character strengths remain the same | same as always |
| **With What I've Got** | you will need to adjust your expectations of yourself based on how your body is feeling | very different |
| **Right Now** | now is the time you have control in your life | same as always |
| **To make the most** | You have the power to maximize your benefit | same as always |
| **Out of today?** | Living life is a day to day process. One good day can lead to another. | same as always |

**Now You Try It!** As you work with this concept use the Day Tracker Form to keep track of where you fall on that 0 to 100 scale each day. Give it your gut reaction and don't worry about being precise. Also make note of how you judged your day (was it a good day or a bad day?) and see if it matches how much energy you had (75% or 35%?). The important thing is to become more aware of the energy that you bring to each day. Feel free to make as many copies of this weekly form as you need. As you notice the connection between your energy and how you rate your day you will be better able to use the 5-Part Question as your guiding principle as well.

| **Day Tracker** | **My Energy Level** (Check One) | **Day Rating** (Check One) | | | | |
|---|---|---|---|---|---|---|
| | Pick a number between 10 = Low Energy 100 = High energy | Great | Good | Average | Poor | Awful |
| Sun | | | | | | |
| Mon | | | | | | |
| Tues | | | | | | |
| Wed | | | | | | |
| Thurs | | | | | | |
| Fri | | | | | | |
| Sat | | | | | | |

*Chapter 11*

# HAVE A PLAN – FOLLOW THE PLAN

To help us illustrate this next concept please welcome our final client example, Clara. Clara was a 45-year-old married nurse with three kids, aged 10, 13, and 16. She and her husband, Barry, both worked full time. Clara was also very actively involved in her neighborhood and church communities. She loved her job and was planning to work full time until all three kids were through college. Her plans had to change, however, after a routine mammogram found a 5-millimeter lump in her left breast. The radiologist referred her to an oncologist who ran her through a bunch of tests and procedures. All the hurrying up and waiting caused a lot of stress for Clara and her family. Eventually she found out that the treatment plan would include chemotherapy, surgery, and radiation in order to afford her the best long term survival option. Clara knew that she needed to work to help support her family, but she also realized that her treatment would interfere with her job, her volunteer work, and her ability to give her children (and Barry) the attention they needed and deserved. Since she couldn't go without treatment, she knew she needed to come up with a plan that would work for both herself and her family.

The ideas of this chapter build off the concepts outlined in Chapter 7 with the Coping Plan. For this aspect of planning, however, I want to emphasize the specifics of the planning process. Have a plan and follow the plan sounds like a simple concept to be sure, but both parts are key to our success. The first part underscores that we have goals we are trying to work toward and are forward focused. The second part focuses on the steps we need to take along the way to get us to that goal. In some cases we have clear plans that we are working on, like going to school to earn a credential that will get us a better job. Other times our goals are less explicit, like when we plan to be healthy for the rest of our lives or we work hard to give our kids opportunities in hopes their lives will be better than ours have been. Whether our plans are explicit or not, we rarely think about what will happen if they don't work out. In fact it is only when a plan is interrupted do we recognize how important it was to us. Although none of us think too much about it, we all invest a lot of mental and emotional energy into what is supposed to happen or what we hope will happen. We all expect to have a healthy life, that bad things won't happen to us, and that we will have a happy future. When things are going well for us, we don't question these expectations because the plan seems to be working just fine. When that perfectly fine plan falls apart, however, it is a shock and everything can feel uncertain. Our hopes and dreams develop slowly, over our lifetime, but when the plan breaks down it seems like it all falls apart very quickly. Getting back on track requires first that we recognize that the old plan isn't going to work anymore and then settling in to figure out what the new plan is going to look like.

This planning technique has several key components. First, it underscores the importance of having plans whether things are going well or not. When we need to figure out how to re-adjust our plans and maybe set off in a new direction it is good to realize that we are not starting from scratch, but rather just refining the plans we already have. If we take the time to look at our problem, we can see that there may be several options to choose from, so we are not limited on a one-size-fits-all situation. It can be useful to think through, ahead of time, what some of the possible pitfalls of each option are. If we do that before things go wrong, we will not be so surprised if/when things don't go as we expect. Avoiding pitfalls, all together, is obviously the best option, but because that is not possible, recognizing that we fell into a pit, even after the fact, is still useful. That awareness will help us get out of the current pit, and hopefully learn how to avoid others in the future! Having a plan, a head of time, allows us to feel less anxious as we approach any situation, because we know we are more prepared, no matter if things go well or not.

Medical challenges like Clara's are spot-on examples of when this coping skill is crucial. Clara had the plan--or expectation--of being healthy, helping support her family (in every sense of the word), and being involved with her community. That was working well until she got the mammogram results. Typically, with cancer treatments, people feel the most stress during the period between the radiologist saying, "I'm sorry to say we've found something on your scan, you need to talk with an oncologist" to the time that oncologist says "we've done all the tests, we know what type it is, and here is the plan…" This span of time can last a week or more and is the most difficult because that is the period of maximum uncertainty. The power of having a plan is seen in the relief most people feel when they hear what the treatment is, when it is going to start, how long it is going to last, and what the common side-effects are going to be. It might seem like hearing about a plan involving chemotherapy, radiation, surgery, and medication would be overwhelming, but in many cases the opposite is true. As is typical, Clara felt relieved to have a detailed plan, because it was better than not knowing what was going to happen next. That is not to say that she was glad she had breast cancer or that she had no anxiety about what the process was going to feel like, but rather that she knew more about what to expect. She felt more in control over how she would respond, even though she did not have any control over getting cancer in the first place. The treatment plan allowed her to talk with her boss to arrange for time off because she knew when her treatments were going to happen. It allowed her and her family to know when to reach out to their community and arrange to get the support they would need--such as meals, school pick-ups and drop-offs, and help with errands. Before treatment even started, Clara went through a "chemo-teach" session where she and Barry learned about what to expect in terms of side-effects, and what she could do to combat them. She met with a social worker to fill out the short-term disability forms she needed to take time off from work. She and Barry met with me to talk about how to prepare themselves and their children mentally and emotionally. They learned about the importance of how to think about setting schedules and keeping routines as regular as possible. They learned about the normal emotional rollercoaster that comes during different phases of treatment, so they could be prepared when Clara was not feeling physically, mentally, or emotionally at the top of her game. She also met with a nutritionist to learn about how to eat when she wasn't hungry (timing and portion control) as well as what foods would help keep her strength and energy up. All this information gave her tools to make a daily plan that would help her, and her family, get through the treatment process. Obviously having that plan did not reduce the side effects of the chemotherapy or stop the disruption of her daily life, but it did make the ordeal more tolerable because it helped Clara feel less helpless. Once she was done with treatment, she asked for a new plan to help her handle what was coming next: "survivorship." Returning to "life after cancer" can be almost as big a challenge as going through treatment in the first place so having a plan for dealing with this next phase is very helpful. In the cancer program where I work, we designed a class called "What's Next!?" that helps our new patients learn about putting together a plan to get through the treatments and we have one for patients who have finished treatment to help them focus on life after cancer. People have told us that having coping plans allowed them to not get too distracted by the short-term challenges while they were working on realigning what their "new normal" were going to be like.

Although Clara's example relates to cancer treatment, these concepts can apply to any goals or challenges in our lives. A goal might start out as "I want to climb the career ladder at my company" only to learn later that the organization would fail after two years. A goal might be "I need to get in better shape, so I don't get diabetes" until a knee strain from all the running makes that goal change. The first step is to recognize that the original goal or expectation we had is not going work out. This is not as easy as it sounds. We often hold on to goals and aspirations longer than is healthy for us. At the same time it is important not to give up on goals before we have given them our best effort. One of the tricks here is to take a step back from a goal that is not coming as easily as we expect and see if there is a way to refine it. Sometimes taking that step back helps us reaffirm that the goal is the right one but just needs more time. Other times it helps us accept that the goal is not the right one, for us, at this time. Once we are ready to move on, then we get to step two.

The second step involves taking all the energy and effort we had devoted to the old goal and re-focusing it on what our new goals are going to be. We might need to devote some energy and effort to a job search by using the connections we made during our time at the short-lived company. We might want to look for a gym with a pool to switch from running to swimming for our exercise routine. There will be incremental steps that will lead to the new goal so thinking them through will help us make the plan. As we refine what our new goal is going to be, it can also help to write out the steps we will need to achieve it. This helps us visualize the idea in more concrete terms and the steps can serve as reference points that we can go back to later, to see if we are following the plan as we had laid it out. Once we have it in writing, we should put it up somewhere we will be able to see it every day (on the closet door, bathroom mirror, or the fridge). This will help make the plan a part of our everyday life and remind us of our commitment and dedication to ourselves and our goal.

The daily habits we establish as a part of that plan will help us live up to the second half of this rule, "follow the plan." There will be days when we want to give up on our plan, especially in the beginning.

Struggling to stay with a plan is normal. We all have our "favorite" excuses for why we can't do something. It is important to notice them, but not buy into them. Like all our emotions they are a signal that our current goal is not the right fit. Sometimes the reason we struggle is because the steps we set out for ourselves are too big. "Once I get that new job I will get on the executive board and really show them my leadership skills!" "I think joining the pool will give me that chance to compete in the master's swim tournaments that I've heard about." If we've aimed too high, then we can find a smaller "part-way" step to take that will help us make progress in a more reasonable way. "First I've got to find the job (gym) then I can think about growing in place." Once we have a reasonable plan, following it step by step reduces a lot of anxiety because we don't have to start over from nothing every day. It takes less energy and effort to put one foot in front of the other than it does to constantly be trying to figure out the right direction. As that process continues, the easier it becomes but progress is not always even or constant. We may have days when we "crush it" and accomplish everything we set out to do and other days when we can't seem to get out of our own way. Even if we try and fail one day, we have a new opportunity the next day to persevere. A written outline can help remind us about staying on task and following the plan as we have designed it. The simple building blocks give us back some of the control we know we need. It helps to start with small goals at first and then build from success to success. As Clara found out, having the plan allowed her to get through the tough days of breast cancer treatment and go on to live her life as fully as possible.

**Now you Try it!** When thinking about our current challenges, it is okay to take a step back from the process and reevaluate the goal we are aiming at: is it still the right one? Look at what barriers have gotten in our way, are there any we had control over? If you are stuck right now, do you know how you got stuck? Make a list of ways to get unstuck. Update the planning sheet from Chapter 7 to see how your plan is starting to come together!

| Time | Goal Same or New | Barrier Same or New | Strength Same or New | Next Step |
|---|---|---|---|---|
| Week | | | | |
| 1 Month | | | | |
| 6 Month | | | | |
| 1 Year | | | | |

*Chapter 12*

# THREE RULES OF LIFE

Remember Brad, from Chapters 2 and 3? His story is more common than we'd like to believe. When he came home, he was angry about the life choices he'd made that got him into that situation. He berated himself for not working hard enough to get more construction work or any job that wouldn't have led to permanent disability. When he thought of the future, he saw only hard choices ahead of him and worried about what he could do to support himself and his family.

Brad had lived by the rules he was raised with; always staying on the right side of the law, being a good person, following the tenets of the faith community he grew up with. Unfortunately, following those rules didn't lead to the outcomes he had wanted. He came to question whether the rules were the right ones or whether he just made bad decisions. Since his life, up to that point, had not turned out the way he planned, he wondered if that pattern would continue for the rest of his life. When he came for help, he was not only dealing with his physical recovery, but also struggling to trust his own decisions about what to do next with his work and family life. His relationship had changed with Sarah and the kids, something none of them had planned on or been prepared for. The Three Rules of Life is a technique that Brad used to sort through what he had control over past, present, and future.

**Rule 1: Recognize that every decision requires making choices**. Even a decision not to do something is a choice. "I'm going to sit on this couch for a while" is a choice just as much as "I'm not going to sit on this couch anymore." We all make many decisions every day, some big, most very small, often with little awareness that we are doing so. We decide what we eat, how we dress, or spend our time every day, but we also could make different decisions about each of those things. This may seem like a straightforward idea, but Brad wrestled with this concept, as many of us do, for two reasons. First, he didn't see many choices when he was faced with the job slow-down. He felt, at the time, that there had been no good alternatives to joining the Reserves, so there really wasn't much "choosing" involved. Secondly, he thought Rule #1 implied he was to blame for his decisions because at some level his injuries were the result of the choices he had made. He was stuck in the common dilemma of feeling like he had few options to choose from yet also responsible for the outcome of that decision. This led to a maddening circle of feeling punished and responsible all at the same time. This was one of the first lessons of this technique, and something that is important for all of us to realize. We don't choose what life throws at us, be it a natural disaster, illness, job turmoil, or being injured in a war zone, but we do have control over how we deal with it. Brad was not responsible for the events that happened to him when he was overseas, but he could take responsibility for how he was going to respond to it.

Brad started to combat that sense of being stuck, by seeing that he had control over his small and minor choices, reminding himself that he was not completely without options. Once that basic truth took hold it was easier to build upon it and see that more consequential decisions, based on a collection of the minor choices, were also within his control. This concept is true about present decisions, but it is also helpful in reviewing our past decisions. Reviewing past options allows us to deflate our "all or nothing" thinking and not hold on so tightly to what has already happened and can't be changed. Once Brad thought back over his decision process, he remembered considering going out of state to find work, changing careers, going back to school, as well as joining the Reserves. He would never know how those alternative choices would have turned out, but he could see that his eventual decision was not just a whim. This same thought process was also a driving force in his day-to-day life in recovery as well. He was making choices about whether he would go to physical therapy each day or not, deciding how often, and what, he ate to fuel his recovery. The scope and variety of decisions were not the same as compared to his life before he went overseas, but he was facing up to and making choices just the way he did before he got hurt. He came to see that he was not helpless in his life, even if his body was not able to do things the way it used to. Knowing that choices were going to present themselves, and decisions were going to be made, allowed Brad to see an opportunity to reclaim some responsibility, and control over what happens in his life.

**Rule 2: Recognize that <u>every choice has positive and negative consequences</u>.** This rule underscores the truth that there is no such thing as a perfect choice. Many people feel stuck, thinking that they can't make a choice until they know what the "right" one is, like they want to know ahead of time what is going to lead to that good outcome. Whether a choice turns out to be a good one or a bad one, however, is usually decided based on what happens afterwards, and we can't know what that outcome is going to be ahead of time. The fact that every choice has upsides and downsides was a central focus for Brad. When we talked about the decision to join the Reserves, he remembered weighing whether to stay home, to try to find new work in construction, or try going back to school, or making a career change. A local job had the benefit of being closer to his wife and kids, something he valued more since the separation. The downside was that the pay was poor, and the work hit or miss. He had the option to leave the state and travel long distances to other construction sites. The money in those cases was often better but travel and lodging costs always cut into the money he would make, and it would also take time away from seeing his family. He had no money to go to school, and had never enjoyed being a student anyway, so that option seemed like a long shot as well. The Reserves option came with a nice recruitment bonus, that he could give to his family, and the guaranteed pay and benefits, with clear expectations and timelines, felt more dependable. That dependability was a strong draw, compared to his daily worrying if the current job was going to last, or if there would be another after this one finished. He was aware of the downsides, as well. He would have to go overseas and would be away from his family for long periods of time, which was painful, but since the time and structure was so well defined, it felt more achievable to him. He knew there was always a chance he could get injured, but he was in decent shape and had done well in the basic training weekends, so he felt confident in his ability to take care of himself over there. He was already familiar with managing the high risk of injuries from his work on construction jobs, so the risk of being injured overseas did not seem that much different to him.

After the fact, he wished he had made a different choice. He wished he had had a crystal ball and had seen the future; he wished he had known ahead of time that the upsides of the overseas gig would not outweigh the eventual downsides. Later, when he thought back over the choices, he wondered why he'd made such a "dumb" decision. He regretted the path he chose because of all the negative aspects of his life in recovery. As he talked through the idea that no choice is perfect, he came to see that no matter what choice he made, it was going to have downsides and upsides. He had already seen the downside of not changing; staying at home in a faltering economy had him worrying all the time so he had not been the husband and father that he wanted to be. He remembered being on a downward spiral with things not getting better for him. One of the key steps to getting out of the trap of "woulda-coulda-shoulda" was freeing himself from the idea that he "should have" known what the downsides were going to be ahead of time. Mapping out the different options he had at the time, and the likely pros and cons of each, allowed him to see that there was no "right" versus "wrong" path to take. He would have faced up and down sides of whatever choice he had made.

The fact that there are no perfect choices, doesn't mean that some choices aren't better than others. Drinking a case of beer a day is not likely to lead to good things, no matter how good it tastes in the moment. It is also true that the relative balance of good and bad aspects of decisions are not always apparent, at the moment we are making them, or in the immediate aftermath. Brad struggled, for a long time, to see the upside of the choice he had made. Given his life-altering injuries and how they affected his career, relationships, and parenting capacity, it was hard to see how any of the other choices could have turned out so badly. In the beginning, when he first got back to the States and he was still coming to terms with what happened, the negative aspects of life certainly outshone the positive. It was only over the course of time, that he came to see how the explosion led to a stronger sense of control and character. Sarah came back into his life on a more full-time basis, initially to take care of his needs, but eventually as a partner. They had to learn a different way of interacting and deciding who was in charge of what tasks. He had to learn how to walk again so that he could still go in the back yard and throw the ball with his daughter and walk under his own power into his son's music recitals. These were hard won victories, after a lot of healing and working to get to a "new normal" in his life. To be clear, no one would have prescribed getting "blown up" just so Brad could have these positive outcomes, but the ability to get them at all only came about when he decided to take control of what to do with his options. While most of us probably are not weighing such heavy choices, we should keep Rule 2 in mind when we decide what route to take, which medical treatment to undergo, which house to buy, what political candidates to vote for. Basically, any decision we can think of will have positive and negative effects that result.

**Rule 3: Recognize that making some choice is inevitable**. Every day we are faced with options that we decide between. We are either going to sit on that couch or we are not going to sit on that couch, it's going to be one or the other! When faced with more difficult choices, it is common to want to avoid or defer making the decision to a later time, but "do nothing" or "do it later" are both decisions as well. This was one of the reasons that Brad didn't like this technique at first. He felt the "3 Rules" were a fatalistic way to look at things--like he had been "doomed to choose" with no way out from the beginning. Before he went overseas, he weighed the upside of staying with a familiar job, lifestyle, and routines versus the downside of the stress and financial worries involved in the status quo. After he got back from overseas, he re-evaluated the choices he made through the lens of what the consequences turned out to be. He thought the first rule, "every decision is a choice," meant it was his fault because he had chosen the bad outcome until he recognized that he had weighed that decision based on his best options at the time. Brad realized, with the second rule, that all his options had consequences. Choosing to stay in local construction meant going from job to job, stressing out about when or where his next paycheck was coming from; a pattern he knew too well. Choosing the different path helped him feel more in control at the time. Recognizing that he didn't have control over the accident but he did have control over how he responded to the after effects restored some of that lost sense of control. Finally, accepting the inevitability of making choices allowed him to let go of the fantasy that he could have avoided his "fate" by not choosing what he did. A different choice would have led to a different outcome, perhaps an even worse one. If he had gotten injured as a journeyman carpenter, for example, he wouldn't have gotten the support from his bosses that he did from the military. In his most frustrated moments, he pointed out that it could also have turned out better but, in the end, there is no way to know what would have happened had he traveled down the "path not taken" and he couldn't go back in time to change it anyway.

Most of us, like Brad, aren't even aware of how we continually make choices in our lives. We choose what to wear and what to eat, what route to go when we leave the house, and what attitude we bring with us as we approach the day. When Brad started going through physical rehabilitation, he worried that he was only capable of making bad choices. Every time he looked at his body, he was so aware of the unfortunate outcome caused by his choice to go abroad. All his limitations were front and center when he started, and he had not yet built up the physical (or emotional) strength and healing to be able to see his eventual capacity. As he talked more about these decisions in therapy and practiced what he was learning on a day-to-day basis, he found a lot of comfort in remembering that he had also made decisions that did not end badly. He had always chosen to work hard when he was on the construction sites, coached his daughter's softball team, helped his family when they needed him. He continued to make similar choices in his physical rehabilitation, working hard on his physical, mental, and emotional therapies, to recover so he could get Sarah and the kids back in his life, for example. Those good choices allowed him to have even more opportunities as his strength returned and he could think about what he wanted to do for work and how he could give back to his community. Unfortunately, most of us are not as quick to catalogue our good decisions as we do our bad ones. Brad came to see that his past choices were a mix of good and bad, as were his present-day choices, so he was finally able to see himself in a less judgmental way.

This way of thinking, accepting the "good" and the "bad" choices equally, allowed Brad to not only forgive himself for past decisions, but it also continued to help him make choices in the present. Brad had been a heavy smoker before he was injured, but when he was in the rehabilitation facility, and wasn't allowed to smoke, he used the "3 Rules" to help himself quit. Prior to his injuries he felt that smoking for over 20 years meant that smoking was no longer a choice for him. He used to joke that he should keep his cigarettes in the coffee cup since he couldn't have his first cup of coffee without one and that his truck wouldn't start if he didn't have a lit one in his mouth. Although he often regretted ever picking up a cigarette and he knew all the health problems associated with smoking, it wasn't enough to get him to quit because it seemed like smoking was no longer something under his control. We focused on the how each cigarette he smokes is a choice he can make. No one is going to come along and put a cigarette in his mouth and light it or take it away from him. So, even if Brad had made the same "bad" choice to smoke every day for the past 20 years, he was still able to make a different choice today. He used the "3 Rules" to write out the pros and cons to smoking and the pros and cons to quitting. He also kept track of his smoking habits and routines, so he could see the patterns of when he smoked. These two exercises showed him that he was "choosing" to smoke multiple times a day, and often there were specific reasons why he did. When he made smoking a more overtly conscious choice, he reduced his habit by half. Once he found alternative ways to get the "upside" of smoking (stress relief, routine, quiet time) without a cigarette, he quit smoking all together. By becoming aware of the many choices he made, Brad gained a greater sense of control over his behavior and future choices. Brad used the "3 Rules" to let go of regrets about past "bad" choices and focused instead on making healthy choices in the present, which also set him up to have a more positive outcome in the future. Quitting tobacco helped him prove that to himself and his family.

**Now You Try It!** In this exercise, note the up-sides and down-sides for various decisions. First do this with a past decision, one you've already made, since you know how it all turned out. As you look at the pros and cons do you like the way it turned out? Next, do the same thing with a current decision you are trying to make. You won't know the outcome yet, but you can weigh out the pros and cons just as you did with the past decision. As you compare the pros and cons you will be better able to decide which option seems more acceptable to you. How you weigh them out will include your risk tolerance and your sense of control. There is no perfect choice, only the best one you can make at this moment, with the information that you have. Go for it!

| Decision | Upside | Downside | Outcome |
| --- | --- | --- | --- |
| | | | |
| | | | |
| | | | |
| | | | |

*Chapter 13*

# THE 100TH BIRTHDAY

These next two chapters will focus a little on perspective taking. When we go through hard times it is easy to get lost in the weeds of our own misery. Having ways to restore a healthy frame of mind, that helps us see our own problems in context, can be helpful. This chapter focuses on the perspective of how our current hardships fit into our life as a whole and the next chapter focuses on the way we compare our problems to others. The long term perspective on our own life can be seen if we imagine living to the age of 100.

Having a 100th birthday is not something everyone gets to experience, but as a thought exercise, imagine how you would look back on today if you did reach that age. This was an idea that Clara and I talked about when she was going through her breast cancer ordeal. Clara remembered one day, early on in her career, talking with Dan, a gentleman who lived in the nursing home where she worked. He was mad and snapping at the staff, so she went to sit with him. She asked him why he was upset and refusing to go to any of the activities. He said his family had not come in to visit as he had expected. He was quick to point out that his sisters and brothers were all wealthy, but they rarely came to see him. He felt abandoned there in "the home" because they never invited him to holiday or family festivities. His disappointment about being alone compounded frustration from earlier in the week when his doctor could not find the cause of his leg pain. The more he talked about these recent frustrations he remembered how he had always felt like the black sheep of the family. He got wrapped up in regrets about decisions he had made a long time ago, like dropping out of high school and joining the merchant marines where he sustained his initial injuries. He went on to complain that he didn't care what happened anymore, if his life was going to be like this, he had no interest in it. Clara listened to his regrets, seeing how each one was built upon the ones before it. She went home that day thinking how sad it was to be so miserable, so often, about so much, and she resolved not to end up like Dan.

When Clara first heard she had breast cancer, however, she made some of the same perspective errors that Dan had. She looked to her past, at everything she had done, eaten, drank, or potential toxin she might have exposed herself to, trying to figure out how she could have "gotten it." She read up on causes of breast cancer, looking for which ones applied to her, thinking that some past behavior must have led to her current situation. Many people wish the cause of their cancer had been something within their control because, at least then, it wouldn't feel so random. Clara also worried how she was going to be able to prevent it from coming back in the future if she didn't know how she got it in the first place. Fear of recurrence is one of the most common fears across all cancers, made harder still because there often isn't some core decision like dropping out of high school that could have been avoided.

In our sessions together, Clara recognized she needed to shift how she thought of her cancer if she was going to be successful in overcoming it. She realized looking for the cause of her cancer, in the past, was not helpful since she couldn't change what already happened. At the same time, her story showed her that she had strengths she could still rely on. She had overcome difficult challenges, like surviving relationship break-ups in college, academic stress in nursing school, and managing heavy caseloads at work. So, although breast cancer seemed more life threatening at first, she had the same challenge of learning from the past and not getting swallowed by the uncertainty of the future. She started asking herself, "Am I going regret this decision, will I think this is such a big deal, if I live to 100?" The answer was a resounding "Yes!" when it came to decide about chemotherapy, surgery, and radiation treatments because those decisions had profound effects on her health. It was a resounding "No!" when she thought about getting her holiday cards mailed out on time or contributing to church potlucks while she was in treatment or working weekend shifts when her boss forgot to do the staffing correctly. Her answers might have been very different before she got the diagnosis, but not so when she sat with that longer-term perspective. She also realized that no matter what she had or hadn't done in the past, health-wise, she could certainly make choices today to reduce her recurrence risk going forward. That is not to say that she enjoyed every decision since chemotherapy and radiation are not fun, but she made them, knowing that her disease was treatable, especially if she chose the more aggressive treatments that emphasized long-term health over short-term comfort.

**Now you try it!** Take a moment now and do this thought experiment for yourself. Imagine you have just finished your 100th birthday party and are sitting back to think about your life so far. What would you like to see in your life as you look back on it? Are there things you wished you had done more of? Are there things you wished you had done less of? How would you look back on what is happening today?

When you look at your answers to these questions, you will get some perspective on your current life. The gift of this exercise is that you don't have to "travel back in time" from your 100th birthay. You have the power to prevent those potential future regrets by making these healthy changes now.

It might help to look at what you wrote down on your Coping Planner in Chapter 7. Ask yourself which of those goals you are going to really care about on your 100th birthday. Some of them will deserve the resounding "YES," others may come out as a "MEH," and the rest deserve a resounding "NO." No matter what the answer, you will have a better sense of what goals you want to keep.

| **100th Birthday Perspective** |
|---|
| What would you be glad you did? |
| What would you think you could have done better? |
| What turned out to be important to you over time? |
| What turned out to be a waste of time in the end? |
| Who or what did you wish you had more time with? |
| Who or what did you wish you'd spent less time with? |

*Chapter 14*

# THE LADDER OF LUCK

The perspective error of comparing ourselves to others, also known as the "why me and not them?" question is another popular one. When Clara talked with her friends, she secretly wondered why they hadn't gotten cancer. Clara knew it was not helpful, but she legitimately wondered why cancer had "only" happened to her. She'd had these friends since college, and they had all eaten the same kinds of things and exercised about the same amount. Some even had worse habits than her, so how was it fair that she got the cancer, and they didn't? She hated thinking that way, but cancer has a way of making people feel like their problems are the only ones that matter. It reminded her of Dan wondering why he had the bad luck of ending up in that nursing home, worse off than his siblings, focusing on his helplessness and despair. In comparing themselves to others Clara and Dan were both doing a normal thing that anyone might do, but they were being selective about who they compared themselves to. At first, Clara tended to look at others who did not have cancer, or who had less advanced cases, and feel sad that she did not have their luck. After spending some time at the cancer center, however, she also saw a lot of people who were more ill, so she felt both grateful, for having a less severe case, and guilty, for feeling relieved if they had it worse.

This perspective error is based on the idea that there is only one ladder for ranking how lucky we are, and we are all on it together. Picture yourself in the middle of the ladder, with some people above you and others below you. We don't have much control over where we rank on this ladder, we just are where we are. This is especially poignant in today's world where the consequences of being "luckier" are profound on our health and opportunities. It also contributes to the lie that some people have a "right" to be on the upper rungs, more so than others, and that the only way to move up the ladder is to have someone else move down. At the same time, it is true that we don't all start in the same place, with the same physical, mental, and emotional strengths and the same economic resources and opportunities.

A more healthy way to think about the ladder of luck is to recognize that we each have our own. How our ladder compares to others is determined by a lot of things but luck isn't the only factor. When we focus on the parts of our life that we have control over, we climb up the ladder to greater heights. When we focus on the parts of our life that we don't have control over, we tend to sink down the toward the bottom. When Clara looked around the cancer center, she could see that people's success in coping related less to the stage of their disease, or what body part was affected, and more to focusing on what they had control over. Once freed from the idea that there was some cosmic "good fortune" ladder that we are all ranked on, Clara was able to focus on her own ladder of success. She still looked to see how others were managing their care, but she stopped comparing her "luck" to theirs. She recognized when someone else was coping well and tried to follow their lead and she learned to avoid the mistakes that others were making. She came to see that she had control over how high or low she was on her own ladder.

So, whether the comparisons are based on where we started or how we compare to others, the goal of perspective shifting is to help us focus on what moves us forward. In the end we want to live a life with the fewest regrets possible and to feel we have fulfilled our true potential. Recognizing where we are on our own ladder of life allows us to focus on the acts and attitudes that we have control over. This is true if we live to the ripe old age of 100 or get abducted by aliens next Thursday. As we have learned in prior chapters, we can't change the past, but we can learn from it. We can't predict the future, but we can plan for it. Keeping a healthy balance between perspectives is a way to make that happen.

**Now You Try It!** Try making a comparison list. Think of a list of people that are better off that you and a list of people that are worse off than you. These can be people you know in your life or just people you have read about in the news. What do the people on each list have that you don't? What do the people on each list not have that you do? What strengths do you have that none of the people on either list have? What would it take for you to end up on either list? This exercise brings into awareness the comparisons we make when we judge ourselves. Recognizing where we are on our ladder helps us build empathy for others as well as the self-compassion, we all need to make it through the tough times on our way to the better ones.

| | **Have** | **Don't Have** |
|---|---|---|
| **People better off than me** | | |
| **People worse off than me** | | |
| **Me** | | |

# THE IMPORTANCE OF BALANCE

The preceding chapters focused on specific tools that can work to help reduce the impact of stress. The next chapters focus on the importance of maintaining a balanced approach in our lives. I set these concepts apart because, although balance is a more general concept, it underlies most of what we do in life. I think about balance in terms three main axes. There is a need for balance over time, noting the importance of how we think about the past, present, and future. There is the balance between strengths and weaknesses and between internal and external forces in our lives. In other words, balance is a three-dimensional construct. As you will see, one can shift focus back and forth between strengths and weaknesses and internal and external aspects of our selves, but we can only go in one direction over time. My hope is that understanding the interplay between the different aspects of balance can give you more control over how you use the tools that work.

*Chapter 15*

# THE JOURNEY

Life is a journey and there are many ways to get from place A to place B. Samantha knew this well because she was a second-generation timber industry worker. In the summers, when she was a kid, she used to ride with her father as he drove a long-haul trucking route delivering timber products up and down the North-South corridor. There were many different major routes, state routes, and country roads they could take to get their products to the stores. To make each trip a success, her father taught her how to plan the route, find the stores they needed to stop at, and choose places where they could sleep at night. Samantha and her father had to make sure that they had their bags packed with appropriate clothing, depending on the weather outlook, and whatever else they needed. Her dad was responsible for making sure that the truck was in good shape for the journey, was loaded with the right supplies, and was equipped for any emergency. After they finished all the planning and started out on the trip, Samantha had to be patient because it took a long time to cover the 1600+ miles from beginning to end. Along the way, she and her father passed through many places where they didn't want to end up, not because there was anything wrong with those towns, they just weren't the destinations they had planned on.

When Samantha lost her job, we talked about those road trips as a model for how to get through the stress of the job search journey. She could see that there were many ways to get the job she was looking for, but first she had to decide what her end goal was going to be. Did she want to stay in the industry or start a whole new career? Was she going to stay in town or seek work elsewhere? Once she had an image in her head what she was looking for, then she needed to make sure she was prepared for the search. She gathered all the information she needed from her company about ending her employment and what help they might give in her job search. She had to take some time to explore other options and see if there was something better farther afield. She also needed to include Jessica in this journey to see what she wanted to do. Once she had it all mapped out, however, Samantha still had to take the time to interview for new jobs and wait for return phone calls and emails. Much like her childhood trips, there were many points along the way when Samantha didn't like her job options, or offers in front of her, so she had to keep going to the next one "down the road."

Journeys like Samantha's can be difficult for two reasons: frustration and distraction. She got frustrated every time she came upon a new job opportunity only to find that it was not the end goal that she wanted. There were lower wage jobs that she could certainly do, but she would have to string at least a couple of them together to make the same salary she did at the mill. The higher wage jobs were less plentiful and always seemed to get filled "last week" leaving her feeling literally "a day late and a dollar short." The other difficulty was distraction. She tried stringing together multiple part-time jobs, but found that she tended to lose sight of, and the momentum for, her longer-term goals. She would get so busy working the part-time jobs that she would not have the time or energy to find the full-time job, with a living wage, that she wanted. Her goal could feel out of reach, and she worried that the job she was in at any given moment would be the one she would get "stuck in." Moving on to the next one was also stressful because she had to get back on the road again and trust the unknown. Thinking back on how she handled the road trips of her youth helped her regain a healthier attitude.

The journey story is an example of how to work, and find a compromise, with competing short and long term goals. If we only focus on the present, we may lose track of the end point we're working so hard to get to because of the day-to-day challenges that can distract us. At the same time if we only look at our long-term goals, we may get frustrated because we can't anticipate all the roadblocks that might appear along the way. Healthy coping requires us to spread our attention between the two. We want to arrange our short-term goals, so they build toward our long-term ones. On Samantha's actual road trips, she and her father planned out the destinations along their route, but they also paid close attention to traffic and weather reports so they could adjust their route accordingly without giving up on that day's destination. Samantha learned that if they ignored that information, it was much more likely that their trip would get derailed or take much longer than it needed to. On her work-life journey, Samantha worked hard at juggling both long and short-term perspectives. When she felt like she was hitting the wall physically, mentally, or emotionally with the day-to-day routine she would shift her focus and recommit to the long-term goal of thinking about the kind of job she really wanted. When her long-term goal seemed too far away, she redoubled her efforts on the more immediate tasks that she had more control over, like searching on-line for jobs, going to networking events, and talking with friends and relatives about opportunities. Understanding the occasional tension between short and long-term goals helped her get through the awkward lunches and speed dating-like job interviews, without losing sight of her end game. Being able to flexibly shift her focus between the long- and the short-term goals helped keep her momentum going, whether it was on an actual road trip or on the journey to create her dream job!

**Now you try it!** Building on the work you already did on the planning from Chapter 11, you can now apply some of what you have learned to your own journey forward. What would it look like to go from where you are now (physically, mentally, emotionally, and spiritually) to where you want to be? Make a list of what you will need along the way to ensure your success. What are the people, places, or things that you will need to include to help you be successful? Without trying to predict a failure, think about what the pitfalls in the future might be (usually based on ones you have already experienced in the past) and plan for inevitable setbacks.

| | Where Am I Now | Where Am I Going | What do I need to get there | Potential Pitfalls to avoid |
|---|---|---|---|---|
| **Physically** | | | | |
| **Mentally** | | | | |
| **Emotionally** | | | | |
| **Spiritually** | | | | |

*Chapter 16*

# MY GLASS IS HALF FULL AND HALF EMPTY

There is an old question about whether we see the glass half full or half empty. Embedded in that question is the assumption that people are either one or the other. The implication is that "full-half" people see life optimistically, appreciating it for all it has to offer. The "empty-half" people see life pessimistically, noting only what is missing or unfulfilling. The glass is an example of the internal strengths and weaknesses that we all have that tend to be stable over time. Seeking a balance between the two is yet another aspect of healthy coping.

Samantha recognized that she was one of the millions of people who get laid off from their jobs every year, clearly an empty-half kind of truth. Equally true, however, was the fact that she did not lose her loving partner, her family, or other members of her close-knit community because of the job disruption. In the glass metaphor, we cannot see one half without understanding the other. The line that defines the full half is the same one that defines the empty half. For Samantha, as with many people, it was easy to get lost in the negatives and the "empty half" aspects of her situation, especially during those low moments in the job search when she felt so tired, and a permanent full-time job seemed very far away. This was a big change for her because, for most of her life, Samantha had seen herself as a glass half full kind of person, so she tried to be optimistic about her job search. She also got a lot of support from her friends and family to "think positive" and not to "give in" to the pessimistic thoughts. They all had the best of intentions, but it felt like she would only be telling half the story if she followed that advice. Unfortunately, she was not able to turn her mind off from the facts on the ground: she had no job. That reality led to the worries that kept her up at night, interrupting her sleep, disrupting her life even more. She noted, in her defense, that the negative things she thought about were true: the tight job market, the challenges of not being near major business centers, but it was hard to talk with her friends and family about the "whole cup" because they "didn't get it." In truth, looking at the negative aspects of her life did not make them more powerful or more real, they were real enough as it was. Rather, talking about the negative elements helped to validate how she was feeling. The issues were not just inside her head, they were all around her, and no amount of positive thinking changed the realities of joblessness

One of the keys to coping is not so much whether we choose to see the positive over the negative, but rather taking a more balanced approach to our lives. We can use the "full-half" aspects of our lives to manage the "empty-half" aspects. Samantha started to describe the hard parts of what she was feeling in the context of what was working well for her. She noticed that it felt better to be more real and honest with her support system and they responded better for the same reason. She would tell them about how tiring the road trips to other cities were in the context of how grateful she was for the prepared meals they offered. She used the positive support of her community to offset the negative aspects of traveling to look for work. She found that people were more helpful when they understood the full cup perspective she was trying to achieve.

The idea that using positives to overcome negatives is well accepted, but the system works the other way as well. Samantha had some especially promising days with some excellent prospects, and she was tempted to just hope that would be enough. She learned over time, however, that it was important to keep building new prospects even if the current opportunities seemed like a sure thing. More than once she had been caught off guard by a prospect drying up unexpectedly. Remembering the sting of a prospect falling through, even when a new one look promising, helped her not get derailed by the inevitable hopes and disappointments of the process. The "half full and half empty glass" is akin to the ups and downs we all have in life. When we're feeling at a low point, it's good to remember that we have felt better in the past and will again feel better in the future. This can allow us to have hope in the darker moments of our lives. When we are at a high point, it's good to remember that our lives may have been harder in the past and that we may have tough times again in the future. Seeing the whole cycle of ebbs and flows in our lives allows us to alternate between being hopeful and being grateful rather than depressed by the low points and anxious that the high points won't last. In both cases paying attention to the opposite side of the "glass" helps us live in a more centered and sustainable way.

**Now You Try It!** Take a moment to make note of what your strengths are (personal, familial, social, etc.) as these are some of the full-half aspects of your life that you have. Next, take note of the empty-half issues that have been getting in your way.

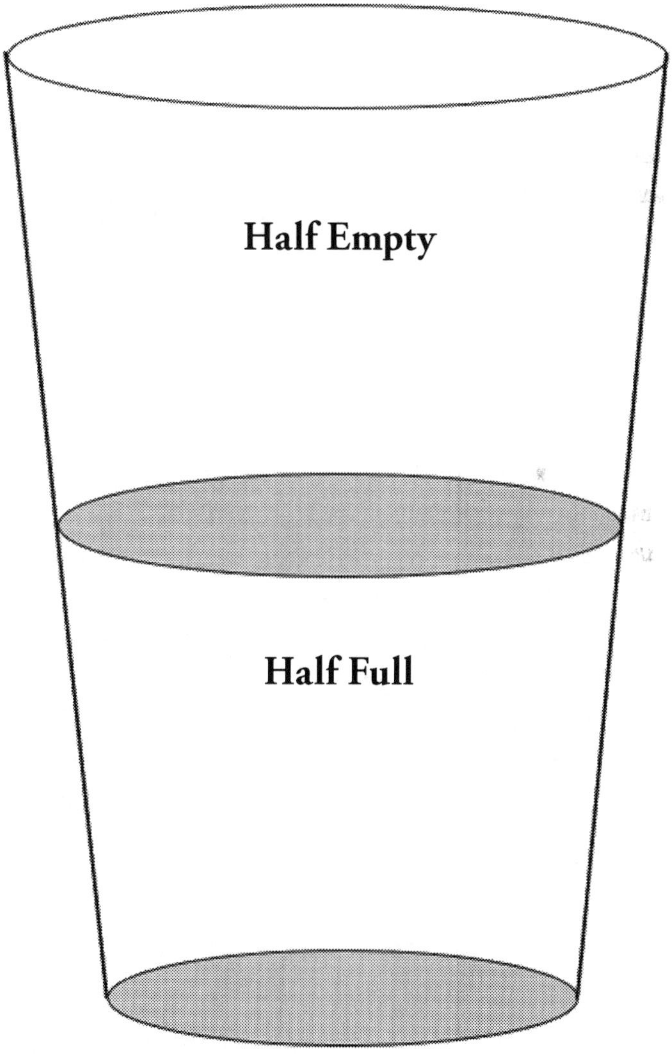
Half Empty
Half Full

*Chapter 17*

# TIGHTROPE WALKING

In Chapter 15, we focused on the balance between our short- and long-term goals. In Chapter 16 we looked at the interplay between the positive and negative aspects of ourselves, and our outlook on life, that tend to be more stable over time. In this chapter we will focus on the balance between positive and negative events in our lives that come from outside us, and tend to be more temporary and variable over time. The "Tightrope" metaphor came about because I used to marvel at the high-wire antics of circus performers who walked across a wire cable carrying their long pole. Not just because I have a lousy sense of balance and I'm not wild about heights, but the act looked effortless. I watched as they crossed the wire, assuming the pole was just a part of the act; showing they could balance and carry the extra weight at the same time. I later learned the pole lowered their center of gravity below the wire as well as giving them the ability to shift their weight from one side to the other to adjust to whatever forces they experienced. That pole was how they "coped" with being on the wire.

Alex faced a similar balancing act when he was first started struggling with the social anxiety. Before he started to face those issues, he had never thought much about how balanced, or unbalanced, his life had been between school classes and the relatively easy social situations in college. The anxiety about the outside pressures came at him like an icy blast of wind and knocked him off that well-balanced life. In the beginning when he was starting to feel all the strong emotions, and didn't yet know why they were happening or what to do about them, he was very unsettled. He had felt in his "comfort zone" doing well in school and surrrounded by people he already knew. He found balancing out the new work obligations and social pressures to be stressful in and of itself. He came in for consultation when he realized he needed a way to regain his balance.

Many of us, like Alex, only pay attention to the balance between positive and negative aspects of our lives after something stressful happens to us. Unknowingly, we all carry a virtual "balancing pole" in our minds, with positive aspects of our lives on one end and negative aspects on the other. When he first came to understand that his mental and emotional life were overwhelming him, he felt like the negative end of his balancing pole suddenly got much heavier. Until he learned more about the clinical aspects of the anxiety, and we began to put a treatment plan in place, he had not been able to get his balance back. The more he thought about all the negative possibilities in his life, the more out of balance he felt. He knew he couldn't just shake off the anxieties, any more than an actual circus performer could drop their pole. These negative aspects were very real and trying to ignore them only made matters worse.

Alex learned there were several ways to restore balance in his life. The first required that he shift his attention toward the negative end of the pole, bringing it closer to him, so he could address those issues head on, lessening the weight of the fear. He did this when he went online to get more information from the Anxiety and Depression Association of America **(aada.org)**, about the latest treatments, local support groups, and to learn what questions to ask his medical team. A second technique entailed putting more weight on the positive end of the pole by devoting energy toward the good things in his life. When he got the treatment plan, his work ethic kicked in and his sense of control improved. He asked for and got specific types of support from his family and friends. A friend of the family, who had suffered with anxiety themselves, for example, gave him names of professionals to call for consultation and advice. He started shifting his thinking about how much weight (importance) he gave different aspects of his life. Letting go of the idea that anxiety was an illness he would never get over helped lessen the stigma when he started to get into treatment. Not holding himself to a sense of perfection about always being on time to appointments or dressing flawlessly helped him get through the worst of the episodes. All these positive steps counterbalanced the fear than comes with the unknown.

To be clear, facing the negatives, or putting more energy on the positives, is not a one size fits all kind of proposition. Physical, mental, and emotional setbacks come in differing levels of intensity, so we need to look for equally powerful counter-balancing forces. So small setbacks (a paycheck isn't coming until next week) only requires a small re-balancing effort (don't pay all the bills this week). A big setback, like a major anxiety or depression diagnosis, requires more heavy support from colleagues, family, friends, professionals, and others. Alex had some experience with this idea already, although he never thought about it in this way. He had grown up as the youngest son of a single mom working two jobs to make ends meet. He had seen his mother balance out many tough situations by using her work ethic, faith, and love of her family. He saw that they did not have less stress or fewer problems than others but he saw how she used her strengths to balance out the challenges. Giving equal weight to the positives and negatives in our lives can make balance possible for us as well.

The idea of balancing works in both directions, although people rarely think too much of a good thing as a problem. One can also get out of balance with too much positive energy, as in the example of people who win the lottery. Having all that money would, obviously, seem like a good thing, but it turns out that the "good times" don't last for as long as we would expect and, over time, the money often becomes very disruptive in their lives. Alex found a similar problem when one of his projects at work had a very successful launch. His co-workers and family were extremely happy for him, and he was very relieved to have completed the project. He knew that he should also be elated, but at the same time, he was thrown back into a period of uncertainty as he did not know what was going to come next or if he could possibly pull off another project as successfully. Rebalancing required understanding that there were always going to be successes and failures at work and that his anxiety was going to come and go accordingly. He needed to keep monitoring himself to prevent a breakdown, focusing on being grateful when projects were more successful and being hopeful when projects were struggling. He put a lot of emphasis on areas of his life that he had more control over, like keeping to a routine, taking his medications, exercise, diet, all of which served as counter-balancing forces to the normal worry about the future.

The last point about "Tightrope Walking" is that balance is not something we achieve and then move on from. It's not like having our 21st birthday, which we only do once. Balance is a dynamic process and something we get to work toward every day of our lives. We may be out of balance for a few minutes, hours, or up to months at a time. We may feel like our lives are in pretty good balance for a period, only later to see that change. No matter how long we have been off center, or how far-off center we are, we can always use these balancing tactics to steady ourselves again. When we can find those counterweights and use them, we get more control over how we cope. Sometimes those counterweights are tangible, like Alex's friends giving him a ride to work, and sometimes they are intangible, like shifting how he thought about what was or wasn't important to him. Working every day to be in balance is what helps all of us walk that tightrope of our lives.

**Now you try it!** Take the list from your "full-half" of the glass and put in on the positive side of the balance beam. Take the list from your "empty-half" of the glass and put in on the negative side of the balance beam. Look at the two lists and see if you feel like those elements are in balance. If one list is longer than the other, then think about what elements you might need on the opposite side to regain balance. For example, think about what new positive elements you would like to learn to counter-balance negative aspects that have been dragging you down.

**Empty Half** (-) **Full Half** (+)

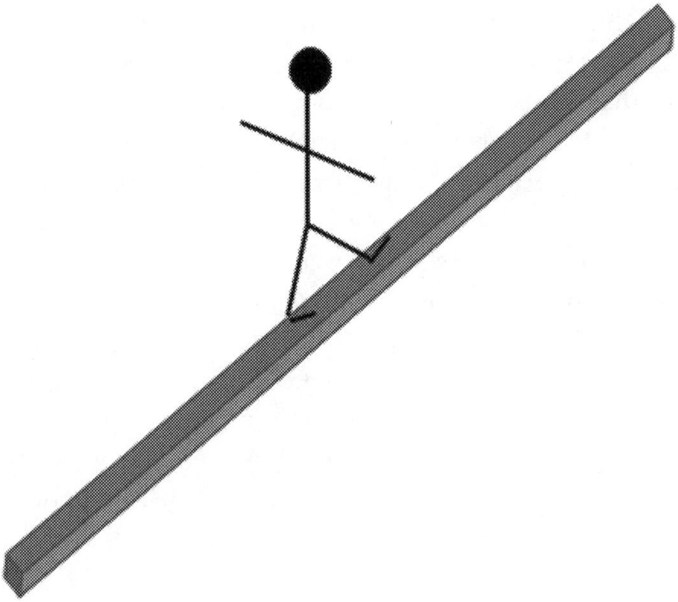

*Chapter 18*

# THE KITCHEN SINK

The final aspect of balance that I want to cover is related to its dynamic nature and the in-flows and out-flows of stress. The kitchen sink is a technique that helps put the ideas about balance into practice. In a perfect world, water comes into the sink and water flows out. Under normal conditions, the sink doesn't overflow because all the water that comes out of the faucet goes down the drain. Overflows happen for two reasons: either the drain is blocked, or the flow of water is too high. If the drain is blocked, then even water dripping in slowly will eventually fill the sink and overflow onto the floor. If the waterflow is too high, then the drain will not be able to keep up and the water will splash over onto the floor as well. Preventing overflows can be done by either reducing the amount of water flowing in or increasing the amount of water flowing out (or both). Stress is like the water. Feeling overwhelmed happens when we have too much stress coming in and not enough stress going out. The kitchen sink metaphor helps us see that we can work to reduce the amount of stress coming in at us and we can also work to "drain away" the stress we can't prevent. Building upon the balance metaphor from Tightrope in the last chapter, the total amount of flow is not the issue so much as the balance between in-flow and out-flow.

Eliot used this metaphor to help him cope during in the early stages of facing his Parkinson's disease. In the beginning of the process, when there were so many changes, he felt like it was all more than he could deal with. Going to multiple medical appointments, juggling his work schedule, thinking about how to change his life plans, all led him to feeling "flooded." One of the things that made coping with the Parkinson's especially difficult was that Eliot had never thought about how he had managed his stress in the past. He worked hard to get through high school and his four years in the Marines just like he did when he first joined the DPW. He often worked non-stop, not sleeping enough, or eating in a healthy way, but he could do it for long periods of time and he had always been able to make the extra effort when the pressure was at its worst. Eventually he needed to crash but he never saw that as a failure of managing his stress. By contrast, facing all the health care decisions, on top of the job demands, left him without enough energy to adjust to work screw ups or changes in his schedule. Prior to being diagnosed with Parkinson's, his usual routine of stress relievers included hiking in the back country, target and skeet shooting at his gun club, time with his friends, and regularly talking with his kids. He didn't feel like he needed any other stress relievers because he drained off his stress as it happened, so his emotional coping capacity (his "sink") never overflowed. When his physical limitations started to add up, however, he couldn't do his usual routines. The quantity and the difficulty of the stressors that come with a diagnosis like Parkinson's were also more intense, so he had the double whammy of too much stress coming in and not enough ways to drain it off.

In therapy Eliot used the kitchen sink idea to develop two types of responses to his stress. On the input side, he tried to limit the amount of new medical information coming in at him by spacing out his appointments. He wanted to understand his diagnosis and treatment options, but he could not fully absorb the details if they came too fast or too much at once. He also asked his children to do some information gathering so that he was not alone trying to figure out what to do or what to expect. He made the job changes he needed by hiring new staff so he could delegate some of his responsibilities, he put in the paperwork to take his full retirement and tapered back on his work hours. On the output side, he made sure that he talked to his friends daily and his children weekly to help reduce his stress when it was building up. He got a physical therapist to help him build up and replace lost strength and capacity. He took some art classes at the Senior Center to help him use a "different side" of his brain and keep his hand-eye coordination strong. He joined a Parkinson's Disease support group to be with other people going through the same things he was. He even participated in their "wolf howling" sessions every month at the full moon. This kept their voices strong and released a lot of stress and got them laughing so hard they almost fell over. To be clear, these techniques did not completely "turn off the tap" of stress coming in at Eliot and he could only process or "drain off" as much stress as he had the energy to. Having two approaches to deal with the stress, however, helped him feel less helpless. He realized he had more control over the amount of information coming in at him as well as what he did with the stress that he already had. This two pronged approach allowed him to do more of the things that worked and less of the things that didn't.

**Now you try it!** Use the graphic to write out the current state of what stress is coming into your life as well as the ways you drain it away. Once you can see that pattern, try thinking about ways you might be able to limit that stress coming into your "sink" as well as what new options you could develop to drain off the stress when it does develop. Remember the faucet will never turn off completely so it is all about managing the flow.

**Stress coming in:**

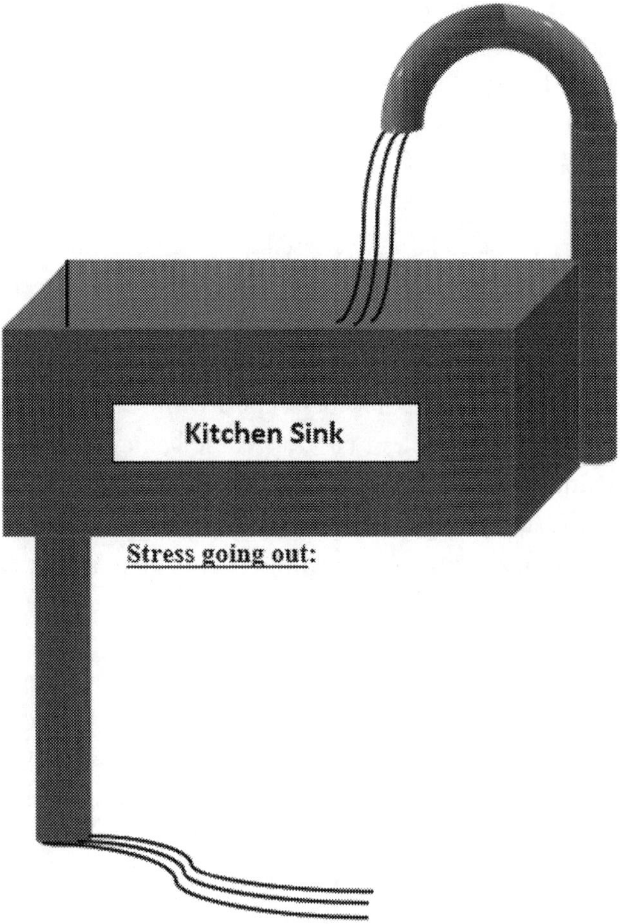


**Stress going out:**

# WRAPPING UP

*Chapter 19*

# PERFECT ISN'T POSSIBLE (OR NECESSARY)

Coping with stressful situations is never easy and can be made harder still if we don't have reasonable expectations. We want a plan that gets us out of the mess we're in and makes everything right. But if the only options are staying with "the mess I'm in" or making "everything right" we end up in a lose-lose scenario. We'll either stay in our current rut or end up feeling like a failure if we miss our goal, even by a little. Setbacks are inevitable in the self-improvement process so one way to keep our head in the game is to not let one negative event shape all others. To combat this kind of all or nothing thinking we can focus on each step of the journey in the same way we think about a batting average or shooting average in sports. Fans of the game know the average is the number of successes per number of attempts taken.

Darlene was devastated when she first heard about her job change, feeling forced to decide between moving up in the company, in a new city, or leaving her job and starting over close to home. She had always worked hard to make her career and personal life as perfect as possible, so she felt pressured to decide how to keep that streak going. The stress impacted her job performance because she was distracted by so many things on her mind. She stopped going out with her friends as much and she wasn't even taking time to work in her yard, which had been her go-to stress reliever. Darlene began to worry that if she couldn't take care of the easy things, how was she going to make a major life change. All the stress made it hard to stay motivated, get her resume out, or feel confident in an interview. She saw herself struggling the way she had when she played softball in college. She remembered the frustration she felt, her first year on the team, when she struck out repeatedly. She knew she was better than that but could not get a hit to save her life. She remembered allowing the frustration to dominate her thinking, going after every pitch hoping to make up for the prior strike outs, only to have more strike outs. In our sessions together she also remembered her batting coach who had told her to forget the at-bats that had come before and the potential ones in the future. The only pitch that mattered was the one she was facing at that moment.

Darlene worked on focusing on the task that was right in front of her, whether that was related to reviewing job prospects, cleaning up her garage, or looking at real estate listings on-line. She worked on letting go of past "misses," like earlier that year when she turned down a good job with a competing firm in town that would have allowed her to stay local. Darlene also kept in mind that "swinging for the fences" was only leaving her exhausted and no more successful. She couldn't be at the top of her game at work while also doing all the real estate and job research she wanted to do, hoping to avoid making the "wrong" decision. She wanted to be her own best batting coach, in a sense. She put her energy into each task, tracked each success and failure, learning from both. She worked hard to repeat her "hits" and avoid more "misses." Darlene came to see that the key to ending any personal slump is to not worry about the slump, but focus on the fundamentals, which she had more control over.

To be sure, this metaphor of a batting average doesn't reflect the reality of the process exactly. In real life we don't have a choice if we are "in the game" or not. We also don't always have the option to be in the "batter's box" or not and we can't know ahead of time if life is going to throw us curve balls or fast balls. Letting go of a perfection ideal, however, is key to focusing on what is possible. Taking risks is less daunting if we recognize any attempt toward achieving our goals is just one of many we will have over time. Slumps are more about our mindset than our capacity, so putting the emphasis on the effort rather than the outcome puts the power back in our hands.

**Now You Try It!** Here is another way to re-think how you're coping with your challenges. Ask yourself: are you putting too much emphasis on getting a "home run" at each step? Is the end goal the only goal? Are you focusing more on the "hits" or the "misses" when you think about how you've done so far? Are you giving yourself enough time on a project to see if it has a chance of success? Use the "batting average form" to track what's working and what isn't. Do more of the things that help and stop doing the things that make matters worse. Let go of perfection to help yourself get unstuck. Take heart in knowing that you will learn from any attempt you make. Play Ball!

**Batting Average**

| What I tried | What worked | What didn't work | What I learned |
| --- | --- | --- | --- |
| | | | |
| | | | |
| | | | |
| | | | |

*Chapter 20*

# HOW TO MOVE FORWARD

The core aim of this book was to give tips and guidelines for how to deal with stress, the universal challenge that comes with living. I presented several stressful situations to illustrate the coping techniques, but they are only a small sample of what can cause stress in our lives. Stress arises within us for many different reasons, both within our own bodies as well as the world around us. The sources will vary across time in our own lives, as well as between us at any given moment. The characters in the stories, although not actual people, were based on real scenarios and highlighted issues and challenges faced by many of the people I have worked with over the years. To help put the techniques in a broader context, I want to share how I think about stress management at a more general level as well.

## Grieving

Based on the chapters so far you might think I am suggesting that the process of coping with stress should be simple. As if we all start from a point when life is good, then something bad happens, we realize life sucks, accept that, look for ways to adjust, learn some new techniques, and soon life will be good again. I wish it were that easy! When we rewind that process and go through the timeline in slow motion we often skip over an important step in the process, the "life sucks" part. Moving forward after a bad thing happens requires letting go of what used to be. Again, much easier said than done. Letting go is a process, like grieving, not simply another task to get done, at a single point in time. There is a ton of stuff written about grieving, so I won't try to capture all of that here, but when I describe the mechanics of grieving to my clients I focus on the emotional energy. I think about grieving as a process of shifting emotional energy from the cherished being, human or animal, place, or thing that is no longer available and re-investing it into new outlets. I think of two kinds of grieving: tangible and intangible. Most of us think of grieving in the tangible sense, as it relates to a specific person, or beloved pet, that has died at some point in our lives. These are tangible losses because our loved one was physically here, and we could hold them and then when they are gone, we feel their absence like a hole in our lives where they used to be. These types of losses are very hard but at least they are clear. We know where our loved one went and that they won't be coming back. The same process also applies to intangible losses, but these are much less clear. Intangible losses are related to our hopes and aspirations. It turns out that we devote a lot of mental and emotional energy to our hopes and aspirations, even if we are not fully aware of it. We invest energy into hopes about our health and welfare, our personal and professional lives, and our family's futures. When something happens that takes that hope or dream away, like we get an illness, lose a job or suffer a break-up, it is a loss. In many cases, we experience both types of loss at the same time. When we lose someone, we have the tangible loss of their presence but also the loss of what we expected our lives were going to be like with them in the future. The tangible losses tend to be less frequent but they are more visible to those around us so we get more support for them. The intangible losses are often known only to us, but are more common, and can range from mild disappointments to the kinds of losses outlined in the stories in this book.

How the grieving unfolds depends in part on how it starts. Some problems come on quickly, such as accidents, natural disasters, sudden job changes, or certain health crises like Clara, Brad, Samantha, and Darlene had. These types of cases are impossible to ignore, and the grieving starts the moment the loss happens. The idea that "everything is going to be fine" dies in that instant. For problems that come on more slowly, like job burnout, relationship changes, or problems that come with age, the moment of loss is harder to define, as Alex's and Eliot's stories show. In these types of cases the loss can be "brewing" for a while and affecting us in subtle ways long before it is evident to those around us. In either case we know there has been a loss once we compare our current state to what we had before.

Once we are aware that the loss has happened, we have to come to terms with what has changed. In the quick onset cases, what has been lost is obvious, since it happens so abruptly, so measuring the before and after picture comes more easily. Acceptance of the change feels less voluntary since it is right in our faces. Brad and Clara, for example, didn't have any doubts about what was different in their lives. In the slow onset cases, the line between before and after is much blurrier and harder to define. As such the acceptance aspect of grieving can come more slowly and we may have to make a more conscious decision about when we recognize the loss of the old way. Alex and Eliot both struggled to see the changes that were happening in their lives and that made finding ways to cope more of a slow learning process.

No matter how they start, or how quickly we become aware of them, however, all problems require an adaptation that takes time. Problems vary in how they play out, with some getting better, some staying the same, and some get worse over time. Some of Brad's injuries, for example, were going to get better with time, medical treatment, and hard work in rehabilitation, while other ones were going to stay the same. Even if he didn't get back to his pre-injury capacity, he was going to improve compared to how he was after the explosion. For him, the tasks of coping required setting and then re-setting expectations as he improved and became more capable and independent. Samantha and Darlene both had job stress that was eventually going to get resolved and then not re-emerge as a problem later so their coping needs were more about learning a set of skills and then, hopefully, being able to move on. Alex's anxiety and Clara's breast cancer were both going to be treated successfully as well but require ongoing monitoring to maintain remission. They both were going to re-visit their coping plans and think about their challenges on a regular schedule, with Alex's psychiatry visits or Clara's biannual mammograms. Eliot's Parkinson's disease is an example of an illness that was going to get more difficult over time, so his coping needs required a similar vigilance as Alex and Clara, but also revision of his expectations, as he lost capacity over time. Although each of their stuations had a unique pattern of how it came on and how it played out, their coping plans were designed to adapt to their unique circumstances as they moved on.

**Hope**

So, what motivates us to make the hard choices we need to make when we are faced with a change, not of our own making? I would argue it is hope. Hope is wanting a better situation and it is a necessary condition to moving forward. At the same time, hope is not a passive activity. As Samantha figured out, just hoping things will get better isn't enough, she had to make the effort to get the outcome she wanted. Where does hope come from? It comes from within us, which can be good news or bad news. The good news is that we have the power to generate hope and we don't have to depend on anyone else to give it to us, nor can anyone take it away from us. The bad news is that it is delicate. If we have tried and come up short in the past, either by our own doing or factors outside of us, hope can fade. One of the aims for this book is to provide the tools necessary to revive hope in those that may have lost it. Hope rests on the idea that what we desire is possible. Hope can be hard to maintain in the face of overwhelming tasks. If we can break up the full task into more doable chunks than our journey can feel more achievable, which will allow hope to be reborn. If we can see progress toward our goals than hope can be strengthened. If we can achieve some of our goals than hope can be realized.

**Persistence**

The final element of the adaptation process requires persistence. We all start in different places with different resources and limitations. We will become aware of our problems at different speeds and at different times and our challenges will each play out as they do, getting better, staying the same, or getting worse. We will either use the coping skills to make us feel better or we won't. What unites us is not any of that. What unites us is the fact that we can create positive change by recognizing that we have choice about how we face our problems. We all can take small steps toward finding a better solution. Putting hope into action requires staying with the program, recognizing there will be setbacks and frustrations as part of the deal. The coping skills laid out in the earlier chapters are designed to be used as often as you need them. They don't wear out or get tired with age. The arc of the story of grieving a loss of what used to be concludes with the arrival at a "new normal" which is not a place or a moment in time. The new normal is a way of thinking, a lifestyle if you will, that acknowledges the reality of what is happening and then works to find ways to make it better.

As my parting thought I want to underscore that we don't have to wait any longer to learn how to cope with stressful situations because there is no one who knows us better than we do. There isn't one answer for how to best manage our stress because there is no perfect pre-made template that will make everything all right. That means we are free to design a coping plan that works for us here and now. The preceding chapters can be used as basic elements of such a plan, the way you would combine ingredients in a recipe. Think about how you want to combine them to make your "good-enough-for-now" coping plan that is unique and custom fit for you. Some ideas will resonate more when a stressful event first hits you, while others may seem more appropriate later once the dust has settled. Coping strategies in a crisis are different than those needed on the long road of coming to terms with what has happened. You have the power to adjust your plan as it unfolds and set new goals as you conquer the old ones. It's my hope that you found what you needed within these chapters and can begin to see a path forward. I wish you all the best in that journey.

Take a moment now to fill out the same stress inventory that you filled out at the beginning of this journey. After you have completed it turn back to the beginning of the book as see how your answers today compare with what you felt when you did it the first time.

| Sources of Stress (Specific) | Not at all Stressful 1 | Kind of Stressful 2 | Clearly Stressful 3 | Majorly Stressful 4 | Severely Stressful 5 |
|---|---|---|---|---|---|
| **Physical health (illness, injury, disease, capacity, endurance, resilience)** | | | | | |
| | | | | | |
| **Mental Capacity (memory, attention, concentration, thinking, focus)** | | | | | |
| | | | | | |
| **Emotional Health (worry, sadness, anger, frustration, anxiety, depression)** | | | | | |
| | | | | | |
| **Spiritual Capacity (faith, spirituality, connection to a higher power)** | | | | | |
| | | | | | |
| **Partner relationship (spouse, partner, boy/girlfriend, best friend)** | | | | | |
| | | | | | |
| **Family Relationships (parents, siblings, extended family, in-laws)** | | | | | |
| | | | | | |
| **Social Relationships (friends, neighbors, colleagues, acquaintances)** | | | | | |
| | | | | | |
| **Community relations (neighborhood, village, town, city, region)** | | | | | |
| | | | | | |
| **Environment (pollution, access to nature, urban, suburban, rural)** | | | | | |
| | | | | | |
| **Work (stability, income, unemployment, obligations, responsibilities)** | | | | | |
| | | | | | |
| **Financial (monthly bills, medical debts, short-term and long-term savings)** | | | | | |
| | | | | | |
| **Other (anything else that you can think of that causes you stress)** | | | | | |
| | | | | | |

**What got better?**

**What got Worse?**

**What turned out to be strengths?**

**What turned out to be weaknesses?**

*Chapter 21*

# THE COPING PLAN

Now that you have more tools and the insights you can begin to put together a coping plan that will work for you. Any area of stress that scored a 4 or above could easily be a target for defining a goal. If you want to pace yourself, you can also take any issues that score a 2 or 3 and see if you can find some ways to reduce the stress in those areas.

Define your goals

What Barriers are in your way now?

What strengths do you want to bring to bear on those barriers to overcome them and get closer to your goals?

**My Coping Plan**

| Time | Goal | Barrier | Strength | Next Step |
|---|---|---|---|---|
| Week | | | | |
| 1 Month | | | | |
| 6 Month | | | | |
| 1 Year | | | | |

# APPENDIX

**Some other techniques**. The concepts described in this book, so far, have all been focused on how we think about stress, which makes sense since how we think most often determines how we feel emotionally. Using these strategies every day is a way to feel more empowered and in control of how we respond to the effects of the stress. Techniques that focus on thinking are great for sure and without them this wouldn't have been much of a book, but I also want to give a shout out to some other strategies that can apply to anyone, no matter what the source of the stress may be.

**Breathing Relaxation**: There has been a huge amount written about the value and benefits of taking long slow deep cleansing breaths. The techniques date back centuries and are part of yoga, meditation, and mindfulness. My more simplified version is summed up by doing the following:

**Blow out your Birthday Candles**

The basic idea is, the moment you become aware of the stress building up in your body, you simply exhale. We all feel our stress somewhere in our bodies. Some people notice a knot in their stomach, some notice a tightness in their chests, some people notice muscle tension in their shoulders, or racing thoughts. No matter where you feel the tension in your body, the result is we don't breathe as deeply as we could. The lack of full exchange of oxygen in the lungs makes us feel more anxious, so it can become an escalating process. When we exhale, we push out all that stale air from our lungs and then a bunch of things happen automatically. We breath in the same amount of fresh air into our lungs as we breathed out, with no conscious effort on our part. That puts more oxygen into the blood stream (the purpose of the lungs) which flows from your head down to your toes and everywhere in between. When the brain senses more oxygen in the blood, it sends a signal to the arteries and veins to relax and become larger. When the "pipes" are more open, the heart doesn't have to pump as hard to get the blood to go around the body. So, your muscles will feel more relaxed because they are getting more nutrients and your heart rate will slow down as it is easier to get the blood to move. Again, this is an automatic response baked into our DNA, so it requires no additional effort on our part. It will only take about 3 to 5 long, slow, deep breaths out and in to start to feel the physical effects. For bonus points, (and who doesn't want bonus points), we want to think only about the air. Picture the air coming in through your nose, pay attention to your chest filling up, then watch your stomach pushing down, and feel the air coming out of your mouth. This helps focus your thinking on one thing that you have control over right there and then. This technique takes advantage of a quirk of our brains that it is easier to choose to focus on one thing than it is to try to ignore multiple other things. Trying to put something out of our thoughts requires us to keep that thing in mind so we don't forget what we are trying to ignore! I tend to emphasize this technique with my clients because it is portable. I am totally in favor of all the meditation, mindfulness, and yoga interventions that folks do, but in the middle of the night or during a busy workday it is not always possible to go to a yoga class or clear ones' mind to meditate. This breathing exercise can be done anywhere, anytime and ultimately is completely within our control. Use it early, when the stress is just starting, and often, as practice makes us better at it. If you like the exhaling, then you might find stepping up to a more dedicated meditation practice will be possible later on. There are also many apps for your phone or written scripts to deepen this practice so I encourage everyone to learn what techniques and audio, or visual, aids can bring this technique to life. Search relaxation breathing practices on-line and you will have a life-time's supply of different options. Try a few different ones and use the one that fits your habit the best. But when all else fails, just blow out those candles.

**Nutrition**: As the old saying goes, we are what we eat. While there is not enough space in this book to do this topic justice either, I just wanted to make a point here that how we feel physically is often a result of the diet routines that we have. If you have been having a lot of physical symptoms, like pain or fatigue, having a look at how and what you are eating might be very helpful. In general, according to the Center for Disease Control [2], healthy diet tips include eating more fruits, vegetables, whole grains, and fat-free or low-fat milk and milk products, lean meats, (poultry, fish), beans, eggs, and nuts. Staying away from saturated fats, *trans* fats, cholesterol, salt (sodium), and added sugars can also go a long way toward helping you feel better. Portion control and adjusting snacking may also be good tips depending on your situation. Because we are all different, however, ask your doctor for a referral to a nutritionist or dietician. They will be able to help you develop a plan with healthy habits and routines that will build a strong foundation for your wellness. Many people in my practice gripe about diets having too many rules and restrictions so be up front with the nutritionist or dietician that you speak with about what your limits are and that you want to start small and work your way toward the optimal diet.

**Exercise**: Use it or lose it, another old saying, also has more value than we often give it. Exercise has been shown to increase alertness, reduce illness, and speed healing, reduce the risk of cancer

---

2 https://www.cdc.gov/healthyweight/healthy_eating/index.html

and increase the effectiveness of most medical treatments. Again, search for "exercise benefits" on-line and you will get millions of hits on the positive aspects of exercise. The Department of Health and Human Services (HHS) also has resources about diet and exercise that focuses on the latest research and benefits (**https://health.gov/**). My only addition to that robust literature is that you should take credit for any kind of movement that you do. Walking to and from work counts, as does doing chores around the house, basically anytime you are moving, you are exercising. There are specific guidelines for each age group (children, teens, adult, elders) but in general anything is better than nothing. Also, in the context of stress management, using exercise to vent off emotional energy (just like Brad did in Chapter 3) is an additional benefit. Again, get a physical exam and direction from your primary care doctor about what kinds of exercises are safe for you and maybe even work with a trainer, or someone who just has more experience, to guide you in what types of exercise are going to be healthy for you.

**Emotional Support**: In addition to this book, there are other ways to get help in dealing with your stress. I would not be much of a psychologist if I didn't put a plug in for counseling of some sort. If you feel like your stress is more than can be managed on your own there is no shame in getting advice and guidance from someone who is outside the situation. In many communities talking about feelings is seen as a weakness but as I noted in the introduction to this book, feelings and emotions are normal parts of the human experience. If you are alive, you are going to have thoughts and feelings. When those thoughts and feelings feel like too much you don't get bonus points for suffering alone. The variety of emotional supports can range from individual therapists that just talk with you one on one, to couples' therapists and group therapies as well. Pastoral counselors and clergy are also skilled in listening and helping find resources in your community. Each one has pros and cons, but one of the most important variables is whether you connect with the person you are working with. When you meet them, interview them to see if they are a good match for what you are looking for. If you don't already have someone you trust to ask for resources, another way to find a provider near you is to contact the psychological association in your state (your state name- "psychological association") or the social worker association (your state name-"social work association") or the psychiatric association (your state name-"psychiatric society") and the same can be done for mental health counselors as well. Search for what you are looking for since they often will have a list of providers in your area. Another way is to call your insurance company or check out the insurance company's website and get a list of providers that already accept your insurance and you can sort the list by people close to where you live or work. If you are working for a company that has Employee Assistance Programs, they also have resources for emergency supports and a list of available community resources as well. All these tips can serve as additional tools in your toolbox, and you should add them to the lessons learned in the earlier chapters in the book and use them as you see fit.

# ACKNOWLEDGMENTS

First of all, I want to thank you, the reader, very much for taking the time to read this book and to aspire to make the changes that you deserve in your life. I wish you all the best in your journey.

I would also like to thank all the people I have worked with over the years, who allowed me into their lives, and taught me so much about being brave and stalwart in the face of great challenges. I tried to honor their journies with the characters and stories that form the backbone of this book.

I would like to thank my initial editor Joan Liebmann-Smith, PhD who saw promise in the original drafts and helped me, more than words can say, create something real, out of a real mess. I also want to thank my excellent reader/advisor Julia Shepard Stenzel, MBA who also saw promise in what I was trying to say and gave terrific advice and guidance in bringing the book to the shape it is in today.

I want to thank everyone at Balboa Press who were willing to take a risk on this first-time writer and gave me the structure and support that allowed this book to go from a file on my computer to a book in your hands.

I want to thank both my parents Anne and Ned Bullis for the guidance and nurturing they gave me over the full course of my life. They should know I am the man I am today thanks to them.

I would like to thank my children Thavy and Nira for loving me and being such a source of joy in my life and for being a guiding light in my own growth as a human.

Last, but the farthest from least, I want to thank my wife Kay for being my best friend, colleague, and partner in life, without whom none of this would be possible.